The Gifts
of the
Small Church

Jason Byassee

Abingdon Press
Nashville

More praise for *The Gifts of the Small Church*

"*The Gifts of the Small Church* is itself a wonderful gift. I couldn't put it down. From 'The small church is God's primary way of saving people' on the first page, to the imposition of ashes on his infant son's forehead on the last page, I smiled, laughed, nodded in agreement, and shed a tear or two as I read. Jason Byassee has written a touching, wise, and important love story about a quiet but incredibly important institution in our culture: the small church."
—John Buchanan, Editor and Publisher of *The Christian Century*

"Jason Byassee is almost too young to be this wise. But don't be fooled: this enchanted little memoir is packed with the wisdom of an old soul. Without nostalgia or hagiography, and with verve and wit, Byassee shows us why God continues to inhabit that forgotten place which is the small church. Despite the 'bigger is better' mentality of America's polished Christianity, he convinces us that God thinks small. And his prose has the same simple beauty as the churches he celebrates. This little book, like those small churches, is what Raymond Carver taught us to call 'a small, good thing.'"
—James K. A. Smith, Calvin College

THE GIFTS OF THE SMALL CHURCH

Copyright © 2010 by Abingdon Press

This book is printed on acid-free paper.

Library of Congress Cataloging-in-Publication Data

Byassee, Jason.
  The gifts of the small church / Jason Byassee.
    p. cm.
  ISBN 978-0-687-46659-7
1. Small churches. I. Title.
  BV637.8.B93 2010
  254—dc22

2010004969

Scripture quotations are from the New Revised Standard Version of the Bible, copyright 1989, Division of Christian Education of the National Council of Churches of Christ in the United States of America. Used by permission. All rights reserved.

10 11 12 13 14 15 16 17 18 19—10 9 8 7 6 5 4 3 2 1
MANUFACTURED IN THE UNITED STATES OF AMERICA

For Tim, James, and Will

Contents

Where the Local Church Is the Solution

In most conversations in which I find myself, the local church is the problem. Clergy complain about their churches like everyone complains about the people who sign their checks. Seminaries complain about churches ("They're sending us the wrong people—poorly catechized, educated, we have to start over from scratch here") just as the local church complains about the seminary ("Who are these liberals who won't work hard or preach in the trailer park anymore?")

Liberals complain about the local church because it's not near inclusive enough. It doesn't mobilize for ministry like it should. There are poor people out there hungering, literally and physically, and we're arguing about whether to have slate or hardwood floors, like some sort of country club.

Conservatives complain about the local church too. They let gay people join. They aren't orthodox enough. They produce the wrong kind of thinking. We are dispensing the grades here, and if you're lucky, you'll get a D+.

From all sides the local church feels squeezed. The church growth people have formulas for how to be great big. Just do this, add that, a squeeze of the other, and you can grow great big too. And big churches are nice—they pay more than their share of what we give in missions, they set the leadership agenda for the rest of the denomination. So ambitious young ministers (like myself) want not just to be in them. We want to lead them. Set the course. Make things new. Captain us bravely into a new century, breeze at our back, hat tipped just so, battleship cruising along at full speed.

So this little dinky church we got plunked down into to start—it's a problem. It's there to glean what we can and move on up out of.

Wallace Stegner, writing about western U.S. history, says there have been two kinds of people who have moved west: the "boomers" and the "stickers."[1] The boomers go west to make a quick buck—to extract what they can from the land and move on. Gold. Silver. Oil. Water. They don't care much how they get it or what wreckage they leave behind.

The "stickers," as you guessed, are those who move in to stay. They build a town. Scratch out a life, a little culture, even some universities, a publishing house or two, some theater, schools, churches and all the rest. They're there to stay. It's not so much that they're all virtuous (God only has sinners to work with, after all). It's that they're committed to a place that becomes theirs, and they become its, and their fates are bound up with each other.

This is a story about how I went from a boomer to a sticker. The sad part of the story is that I went back to boomer. Not that I meant to—I had to go. We were about to have a second child in quick succession and I needed to find the money to let my wife, Jaylynn, stay home with two kids under a year and a half old. When I went to pastor in Zebulon County I didn't really want to stick. When I left I didn't really want to boom. But we don't really have full control over our future, thank God. A life less planned is better, or so they tell me.

Our church, The United Methodist Church, like lots of churches in America, is fearful for its future. We have good reason to be. The numbers are in decline in every registry that matters: money, influence, social standing, or as a friend puts it, butts, bricks, and budgets. There are things that can be done to stem that. Basic competence helps. Removing rank incompetence does too. Solid theological training is essential. Those things are harder to attain than you might think. Without them—without *Jesus*—we're just another local club. Social clubs are fine. But we don't need Jesus to have risen from the dead to all meet back again here next Tuesday.

As Christianity in the West creaks forward, we're having to find new ways to be God's people. Seminaries, like the one I work at, are trying to be nimbler on our feet, less expensive, fight at a lighter weight. They'll survive. They have to. And they'll survive in closer partnership with the local church—mostly large ones, that have resources to share with them and vice versa. To be a sticker in this environment means you love *these* people. And there is more talent at a large divinity school or a large church than we know what to do with. There is no need to speak ill of these parts of the body (the strong trunk, the sturdy legs, the muscular arms) in order to speak tenderly to the weaker parts of the body (the fragile fingers, vulnerable eyes, the tiny ear bones).

---

1. Wallace Stegner, *Where the Bluebird Sings to the Lemonade Springs: Living and Writing in the West* (New York: Modern Library Classics, 2002).

I offer this book as part of the great conversation now going on about the future of the local church. I offer it as a sincere prayer that small churches like the ones I describe here have a glorious share of whatever future God has for us. You will see I offer it as part of an argument right off if you read Will Willimon's wonderfully cantankerous afterword: "yeah yeah, this is a good book. But it's wrong." I would suspect nothing less of a friend than a good counterpunch. But a third friend who read my book and Will's afterword both surprised me: "You're both right," he said. "We need strong large churches. We need strong small churches. We just need strong *churches*."

Take this set of stories, this memoir of two short years of pastoral ministry, as a sort of narrative argument. I want there to be a book where the small local church isn't just the problem. It might be part of God's solution. No, not "might." It just is. If there's anything good in what I do now, it's because of these small local churches that loved me far more than I deserved. That is, they loved me like God loves all of us.

How to Be a Grandparent

But who am I to be offering this? The child of four grandparents who help explain this story.

We're all church mutts now. Almost no one grows up in one denomination, stays there their whole lives, and is buried there. It'd just be un-American somehow. Plus it's good to have more than just people 'from round here' in the pews. The kingdom is bigger than people like us.

Nevertheless something is lost in this exchange. I saw the local church once where my grandpa Byassee was baptized, worshiped, prayed. He never took me there during his life. He'd long left the place behind. It was in a little farm town in West Tennessee, and he associated that work with long hours, a tired back, scarce and undependable wages. And he was right. Plus, we're told, he was clumsy. His parents must've seen that, so they did what you do with kids who can't even help on a farm: sent him to college. So he left that town and never went back. He worked in business, moved with the opportunities, got fired, started his own company, bought out the company that fired him, retired at sixty and moved to waterfront property in Florida. Not bad.

That little Cumberland Presbyterian Church in Dyersburg, Tennessee, was small. Precious. Empty. I didn't even know who to ask around to show me in, to see if people with my name had plaques on the walls.

He didn't die Presbyterian. He died Baptist. It was the price to marry my grandma Byassee, God bless her. She made him get full-immersion baptized and everything. So in Florida they sat on the deacon board. Then sat on the committee that hired a popular preacher. Got left off the committee that hired an unpopular one. The new, slicker, more conservative, more bona fide, real God-fearing Baptist pastor was gonna have an honest, God-fearing altar call every Sunday by God. So every Sunday, with every eye closed and every head bowed, you were supposed to raise your hand if you *knew*, for certain, you were going to heaven.

They did for a while. Then they quit. "I know I'm going to heaven," she'd say. "Why do I need to tell him?" By the end she was the frail little thing inching over to whatever door *he* wasn't at. When grandpa died the funeral home director did the awful eulogy. I sometimes think its being so bad was what made me think "I could do a better job," and sent me into the ministry.

When grandma died, ten years later, I was ready. I did hers. It was enough to make the little town of Meta, Missouri (pronounced "Missoura"), that she once couldn't wait to get out of, look a little good. But how could she have stayed? Everyone else left too—scattered to Boston and St. Louis and other places. Who could blame them? Opportunities, schools, culture.

You don't need to ask if they go to church, do you?

A third grandparent, my grandmother Gode, grew up in Oklahoma as a Methodist. But not *real* Methodist. Religion was for children, not intellectual adults. So the children got dropped off for Sunday school. When they were old enough they could decide whether to go or not.

Any trouble guessing what they decided?

Her dad sold cars. It was the American dream: he drove a new one home every night. For fun they'd fill up the car on hot summer evenings and roll down every hill they could find to cool off. She married a war husband. He went off and left her with three babies under three. He was married to someone else before the third turned one. She raised them alone, unsupported, and spent lots of nights sobbing. My uncle remembers, as his earliest memory, his mother crying over bills she couldn't pay. That'll have an effect on you.

And where was that church? The one she was given the choice of leaving? Hard to blame the church. They never had a chance to know her. What's to blame is the idea that kids should get to decide whether to go or not.

The fourth grandparent. I don't even know what to call him. I never knew him enough to come up with a formal name, let alone a nickname that would express any intimacy. Wouldn't you know this one outlived all the others? I met him once, maybe twice (there's some dispute). I tried to reconnect with him when I went to seminary and started to learn about forgiveness. I called him up on whatever continent he lived on. He talked for an hour. About himself. Famous pastors he'd met. Pastors in "our" family line (speak for yourself, man). When I had to go he said, "Maybe next time we can hear about you," I thought, there won't be a next time in this life, old man. It's not grandchildren's job to initiate with their grandparents. When he died he didn't even know he had two more great-grandchildren by me.

In a strange way I don't know whether to blame him. He went off to war, wore a uniform, had ladies throw themselves at him (isn't that what they always say?). Married three of them, lived with at least one more, died broke and alone.

What on earth in Tulsa, Oklahoma, could have given him the resources to say "no"? That he had a bride back home and three small children who needed him like grass needs rain?

The church could have. If the church were in the picture. Ever heard of youth group? The torturously awkward experience of being told "no" over and over and over again? It's good for you. And in seriousness—a church that says your life is not your own. You were bought at a price. You belong to others.

Would it have made a difference if he'd heard that? I doubt it. But he would at least have had a chance. I'm told he freaked out when relationships got difficult. Hit the reset button. Said "*This* time, it'll be different." Only thing is—he brought himself into each of those new "this times."

The church isn't bad practice for that. Learning that this one is the only one God's got. There is no other, better place where the drinks are always free and the waistline is always thin and the smiles are always forthcoming. Someone has to change that screaming kid's diaper. Could you please? All for Jesus.

Something is lost in the American dream of mobility, travel, bigger is better. To be sure, something is gained: money, culture, experience, all that. And something is lost. Something terrible is lost.

My generation is starting to see that. I saw it when I went out to Zebulon County. Here was a place with stickers. Not all for good reasons—some couldn't leave, some stayed because they could run the place as others left, some, God knows why they were there.

But you know what? They made up a room full of stickers. People who knew each other for decades. Who knew how to bear with someone when they're having some bad years, decades, generations even. How to celebrate when someone has a baby. How to teach about Jesus to someone else's kids. How to pay for someone else's operation because they're in a rough patch. How to call out the casserole brigade when someone dies. They know what the boomers don't: people are made for this sort of community, and without it people become less than people.

In short, they were a building full of people like three of my grandparents, and the church they lost and longed for, though they couldn't quite put words to it.

Is it any wonder I loved the place?

Here's what makes *me* wonder, marvel, slack-jawed with awe actually: that they loved me. I was a boomer, passing through, they all knew it with one look at me. And they loved me.

One final grandparent story. Once my grandmother Gode, God rest her, raised those three children, she had a little time on her hands finally. She'd run through a second husband by then, raised another child. And she got to reading. She found her way, God knows how (do we learn the "how" someday?), to Thomas

Merton's *Seven Storey Mountain*. And she went and found a priest. He received her into the Roman Catholic Church.

She even baptized me. Surreptitiously.

One night when my parents had her babysit, she who wasn't sure they would baptize me, took matters into her own hands, so to speak. She took me to the faucet, wet my head, pronounced the name of the Trinity over me, and inducted me into the church, through no choice of my own. When my parents did take me to the local First Methodist of her childhood days (see—roots are long, even when we try and pull 'em up), she didn't say anything to stop them.

How many people have been baptized twice—*as an infant*? I can see my grandpa getting dunked to marry my grandma, as an adult. But both times as a baby? And baptized by a Catholic woman no less?

This story does not end happily. She loved her new faith so much she went to daily Mass. She joined an order. Moved to St. Louis. Gave up everything she had back in Tulsa: friends, connections, furniture even ("I got the sidetables at least," my aunt declares). She became a novice nun. With four children. My earliest photo of her is in her arms at her convent.

They turned her down.

After a year they sent her packing. I have no idea why. Can you imagine the hurt? Rejected by a husband, left alone, she finds Jesus. She wants to marry Jesus in his church as his bride. And his church turned her away. I am tempted to say something unchristian here, but she wouldn't want it.

She even went to Mass every week still. Just not every day. And when she was in town we had to go too. God rest her.

The small, the local, can still be parochial, closed, inward, narrow. It can hurt people. It certainly did her. Again all God's got to work with is sinners.

So that's it I guess. Pastoring a small local church is preparation for working on being one of those sweet little old ladies who loves Jesus and comes to church all the time. Not because the church is perfect or doesn't hurt people, as anyone who has been around even a little knows. But because the church is where Jesus saves his people. It's beautiful. It's worth living in and dying in and being buried out back of.

That's what Zebulon County taught me.

The last time I saw my grandmother was at my wedding. We often lamented that as much as we'd been in church together we'd never communed together. She'd tease me that she couldn't figure out which Protestant church was which. I'd tease her that only the Catholics would build a cathedral in St. Louis like the New Cathedral when they already had one as glorious as the Old Cathedral.

We honored the church's rules even when we found them inane. So I didn't partake of Mass; she didn't come up for communion.

She came up to me at the reception. "Did you see what I did?"

She must've thought I had more wherewithal than I did. I could barely remember where I was at that point, I was so tired.

"I took communion." Now I was paying attention.

"Really. They invited me, I went forward, and took it. Now we're in communion with each other."

Within a year she was dead. And yes we are in communion with each other.

Carol Zaleski quotes a nun friend of hers: start practicing now to be a sweet little old churchgoing pious lady. Because it takes a lifetime to pull it off. With a lot of grace and forgiveness. And, we might add, a church small enough to know your name and notice when you're missing.

Before I thank some people who need thanking I should add some caveats to what I'll say here. I wrote this book out of reaction to how I hear the small local church talked about, and as a pastor of one such healthy church I wanted to tell my experience of how precious such a place can be. I am not at all saying that all such churches are healthy. In a wake-up call for me, as this book went to press, a small rural church was tearing apart its pastor, who is a dear friend of mine. His offense is not at all clear—but a single bully related to lots of church members is teaching my friend a lot about loving enemies. I know of such churches and such situations—and they receive plenty of coverage in books about toxic churches. My own experience was quite different, and I thought it merited telling. A second caveat—I've seen Methodist churches that simply won't close. District Superintendents and bishops do have to tell some congregations when to go to hospice, and as Christians we know death is not the ultimate ill. A student I know was run out to a Methodist church for an internship that had all of three members. "Maybe you can turn things around," he was told. No, he can't. This is one place that should have been euthanized long ago, but someone's willingness to bankroll a pastor has kept it open for no good reason. I'm not saying here then that such a fate should never await a church. It just sure shouldn't to places like we've known.

Trying to be a sticker like I am at a place like Duke Divinity School, I need to thank people here who made this possible. My Duke colleague Lauren Winner gave this manuscript a working over that bruised my ego but improved the book. So did my local writer hero friend Jonathan Wilson-Hartgrove. I'm not jealous that both are younger than me. Really. Thanks also to Joe Mann, Jeremy Troxler, and Rick Lischer for reading the manuscript, making suggestions to improve it, and for encouraging me.

Thanks to Abingdon and Bob Ratcliff for acquiring and believing in this project. I only missed two deadlines. That I remember. Gratitude goes too to editors at *Circuit Rider*, *First Things*, *Christian Century*, and to Raymond Browning, who wrote *Death and Life in America* (Herald), for which I wrote a foreword, and to Hugh Ballou, who edited *Transforming Power* (Discipleship Resources), to which I contributed. As these invitations came to write, and I kept returning to Zebulon County and Beech Grove, I realized I might have a book on my hands.

The churches I talk about here are real places. But their names are all changed around. I'd have nothing to say if it weren't for them. Literally, in this book, or anywhere else I've written. They did not relate to me on the assumption that I would be writing it all down later. Nor did I to them on that assumption. It just sort of happened. As I was asked to write what I thought about various theological and cultural topics I kept returning to Zebulon County. And pretty soon people were asking me to write the whole story as I remembered it. I hope, like Rick Lischer's great *Open Secrets*, to have disguised identities enough that people won't recognize themselves even. And if they do I hope they see themselves portrayed here with honor and love. And if they don't I can't apologize enough.

I'm thankful to my friends who still pastor small churches because they love it. Grace Hackney. John Varden. People who want to show, not tell, that the small church is where God's doing the interesting stuff, if we have the patience to see it. Grace likes to say she wants her church, Cedar Grove UMC, to be an appointment people covet when she leaves (suffice to say it was not when she got there). John wants to stay below the radar so they never move him from his minimum salary post—and nobody even ever gets to covet it. Bless you both. You live what I write about.

Jaylynn and Jack and Sam and Will. Jaylynn has pastored more than I have, thank God, she's better at it. Lots of these stories are hers. All of them we processed together. Jack was born at one of these churches. Took his first step at another. Sam and Will were born into and baptized into big churches. We know the ministers who baptized all of them. They know their godparents who pray for them and send them letters and gifts and books about Jonah and Jesus. They have something of what we lost when our forebears left their little towns. It'll be curious to see what they do with it.

This book is dedicated to three mentors whom I love, whom, if I could be even a little like, I'd feel like this life was worthwhile. Tim, James, Will: how could I be so blessed as to have three mentors like you in one life?

CHAPTER ONE

How'd You Get out Here?

When you think about who introduced you to the Christian faith, my guess is you think of a small group of people. An influential friend, a youth pastor, a teacher, someone in your family. This is likely true even if you came up in a large church. For even in large churches people find their niches, break down into small groups, get in one another's kitchens and living rooms and become friends.

This book is a set of stories about my time as a pastor of a small rural church in Zebulon County, North Carolina. I never meant to be any such thing. It was an unplanned trip. But once I got there I realized the place was beautiful. This book is meant to tell you how.

I'd had *some* preparation for the small, rural church. My wife, Jaylynn, had been a pastor of what we Methodists call a "two point charge" for a year before I took over my own. A two-point charge means two churches that couldn't afford a pastor on their own band together and share one. That pastor preaches in one church at 9:00 and drives to the other in time to preach at 11:00.[1] So I'd been a pastor's spouse for a year. I also attended a seminary that sends students out to lots of rural pastorates for a glimpse of the life they would likely lead as pastors. So it made perfect sense that we were in one.

But my upbringing prepared me for no such thing. As a relatively irreligious kid I got dragged to the big university Methodist church downtown, if I ever went. We were what I've learned to call "Chreasters," Christmas-and-Easter Christians.

---

1. I've heard of charges with as many as half a dozen or even eight points—they don't all worship on the same Sundays. And they're in places most people don't want to live: deep in the mountains, or near the swampy parts of the coast.

Then I had a conversion experience in a Baptist camp on a lake in North Carolina, responding to an altar call. I responded because the counselors loved me, knew me by name, asked after my story, and then told me theirs, and how Jesus was the answer to all our problems. They were right, of course, he is the answer. He just doesn't sew up our problems quite as tidily as they let on. But we were kids, and so were they, truth be told, college kids, who loved us into loving Jesus. It was a first step, one to be glad for.

They instructed us to find a "bible-believing church." I didn't know what that meant, but I knew it probably wasn't the Methodists, and I figured a place called the "Chapel Hill Bible Church" was not a bad place to start. And sure enough, this nondenominational evangelical church taught me to treasure the Scriptures. It sent me on my first short-term mission trips, where I saw poverty firsthand and could not look away. It was filled with blazingly smart people—scientists and professors and business types, plus the college crowd. It's hard to have all that talent without a church of a thousand or so people.

But within that church we had a little church. It was called youth group. And it was big enough that we could do some cool stuff (what I know on this side of the pastor curtain is called "programming"). We went to the beach and the mountains. We had retreats and Sunday school. And we knew one another by name. We knew who annoyed whom, who dated whom, who would tell what joke when. We weren't all the best of friends. But we knew we could count on the bulk of the forty or so of us to be there, same time and place, each week.

Which is more than most of us could say about our families. I come from a family that divorced and multiply remarried, as do many of my peers in Gen X. Ours is the first generation of mass divorce, so we're naturally a little afraid of intimacy. People who made promises to us broke them. This is not to judge any individual divorce, mind you. It's just to say that across a society that has an effect—we grew up hedging our bets, not sure who to promise ourselves to, or who would break their promises to us. But we also longed for community. And we found it in odd places, like youth group. You might not like everybody, but they'll be there when they're supposed to be—like the families we wished we had.

By college I was looking around outside of evangelicalism. I'd learned evangelicals' burning heart for the Scriptures and laudable desire to introduce Jesus to the whole world. I'd also seen some nasty marriages of partisan politics to faith that I wanted no part of, and my world had grown big enough that I wanted some introducing to it.

And at the time I was going to a Methodist church. Why? It's where the good preaching was. And the preacher seemed to love Jesus, preach from the Bible, and want the world to be more like the kingdom Jesus preached. That didn't seem so bad—it seemed evangelical even. I gradually came to see that the mainline, tired and slumping and old as it was, was also a place where I could find the battle lines. It lacked the chaos of evangelicalism, praise God. Plus the

Methodists' seminary was just down the road, they'd baptized me as a baby, had me occasionally as a teenager, and now wanted me to attend their seminary at Duke. They'd even pay for it. And I'd even grown up a Duke fan.

This was not thorough planning, I realize now.

"You don't sound *mainline* to me," one Methodist minister said to me. I don't know how I answered at the time. But he had to be right—I'd come from evangelicals, I wanted to convert people to Jesus, I memorized Scripture for fun, and felt like my college was dangerously relativistic. I also liked my college, and wanted that Scripture studied critically, and wondered if I didn't need a little converting more deeply into Jesus myself. Methodists had been evangelical once themselves; still were, in pockets.

In a way our church, like many mainline American churches, lives off the fumes of the conversions of the Second Great Awakening. Churches popped up all over the South and Midwest in response to fiery, conversion-directed preaching and emotionally manipulative altar calls in the early nineteenth century. Much like the one I responded to at the Baptist camp (since many Baptists still engage in such proselytizing behavior). There are fancy theories afoot about how that and other revivals paved the way for American democracy. I'm not as interested in that legacy as I am in the legacy of churches that dot this country as a result of those revivals. It works like this: your grandparents go forward at an altar call in the woods, your parents benefit from their disciplined parenting and earn a little more money, and then you build a neo-gothic church on your town's main street to show your religion has gotten civically respectable. An evangelical friend of mine says there'll be liberal churches as long as there are evangelical churches to convert and wound 'em. And, as sociologists tell us, when people make more money and get respectable, they tend to leave the soul-winning preaching behind. Something is lost there.

So off I went to a seminary that prepared people for rural pastorates. And I found there a place much like the ones my grandparents left behind. It was wonderful and mysterious, and small and provincial all at the same time. Jaylynn served her two churches for three years, I served my one for two. It was not very long. And then we had to go off to a job where I could make more money.

I wonder now whether the best thing I'll have ever done in my career wasn't those two years in that small rural pastorate. I know for sure that if I ever do anything else good it's because I was steeped in that place, not nearly long enough, almost a decade ago now.

And you know what the crazy thing is? Once I was a mainline minister myself I heard myself preaching sermons that sounded a lot like the ones I got dragged to at mainline churches when I was a Chreaster kid. That is, I'd learned something about Jesus from the very mainline my evangelical self had once lambasted for refusing to share Jesus with the younger me. Apparently they had, and it'd stuck. My first Easter in Zebulon I was pulling a vignette from the big university Methodist church I grew up being dragged to. Why? Because the preaching at

University Church came from the Bible and was meant to convert people and sought to make the world a more grace-filled place. I remember precisely what it was, in fact—the word in Mark 16:7 that could be translated "and" could also be translated "even." The angel tells the women at the empty tomb "Go, tell his disciples and Peter." And the one who betrayed him. And the one who hurt him the worst. *Even* that one. There is a place for him and for all of us.

That was both evangelical and mainline, apparently. And if the combination worked, I wanted in. Still do.

When we moved to Zebulon County people would ask, "How'd you come to be out here?" I'd ask how much time they had. Or maybe I wouldn't yet—I'd give them a one-line joke to indicate I didn't have time. Now I see the answer they wanted was the long one. They'd listen. And that was what I was looking for.

What This Book Isn't and Is

Many books promise to have the answer. They have *the secret*. They will show you how to live your own, personal, *best life now*. They can introduce you to purposeful living. Some of those books sell in the tens of millions. People are desperate for those sorts of answers. And, truth be told, if I had one of those sorts of marketable answers to give, I'd probably write it up.

But I don't. The church doesn't either. We should stop looking for them. They're a lie.

Did that come off too strong?

The small church is not the answer to the world's problems, any more than living purposefully, "bestly," secretly, or whatever else. The small church is just God's primary way of saving people.

Think of the small villages you may have seen in the United States or elsewhere. Local communities on the roadside that we fly by on interstate highways have a small church at their heart. Imagine the standard European village, however small. Now try and imagine it without the stone chapel as its nerve center (it may now be a bar or a B&B, but bear with me). If you've been privileged to travel to the non-Western world, in Africa or Latin America, imagine the villages you've seen without a church in the middle. Even if that church was a hut, or doubled as someone's house. And I'm guessing that it's not shuttered like our small churches here or rehabbed like many in Europe. Megachurches and suburban churches are well suited to an age that likes things fast and professional and suburban. But most of us through most of time have met Jesus in small churches. The great diversity of Christ's body through time and space has proliferated in the small.

And this is no accident. Break open your New Testament to the letters of Paul and others and you will find letters written to small churches. Specific people are mentioned by name. Spats between individual church members are made public. Paul can even ask recipients to bring his personal items to him: "When you come, bring the cloak that I left with Carpus at Troas, also the books, and above all the parchments" (2 Tim 4:13). Can you imagine such instructions being read from the ginormachurches in Barrington or Orange County or Houston, while millions watch from home? Paul here is more like the pastors of rural churches where announcements can go on, and on, and . . . and can get unbearably quotidian and personal.

One Sunday a parishioner interrupted my wife's sermon. *Her sermon.* Jaylynn was preaching away about whatever it was and Janet stood up. "Jaylynn, I've made a mural of photos of the veterans for Veterans Day, and I want to make sure everybody sees it." Jaylynn rolled with it. "Thanks, Janet, we'll be sure we remember." Janet smiled, satisfied, and sat back down for the rest of the word preached.

How could anyone forget?

By contrast think of Willow Creek, the first of the uber-churches where my fellow small-church ministers pilgrimage regularly, encouraged by denominational officials who want their own McCongregations someday. I complimented a pastor at Willow one Sunday in Chicago that the announcements were so tight. "Three minutes, twenty seconds," he said. What? "That's how long they were today. A little longer than we like, but not bad."

They have the service timed. To the second. That's the quality people expect, if they're going to show up in the tens of thousands. How polished. And how different from Paul's churches or those of Zebulon County.

After the admonition for the coat from Timothy, Paul continues, "Alexander the coppersmith did me great harm; the Lord will pay him back for his deeds." Such public airing of dirty laundry sounds more like Janet interrupting the sermon (maybe to tell of someone *else's* misdeeds) than Willow Creek to me. We're not even sure Paul wrote those words in 2 Timothy, but don't bring that up at Willow. At a small church we're used to such messiness.

Not to dump on *suburban* churches generally, or even large churches necessarily. Not all suburban churches are gigachurches, by any stretch. Jaylynn also pastored a small church in suburban Chicago once. Tabor, Illinois, had been a rural town once. Still was, really, it was just swallowed up by suburb at some point. And Tabor United Methodist Church was still small. Most of the people going there in 1950 were still going there when we were there in 2005. It had been an overwhelmingly Catholic town at one point, as still evidenced by St. Michael the Superarchangel Church a block away. Our older members remember their children being raised in town being referred to by the Catholic kids as "the publics"—it was that unusual in such a Catholic town to go to public school.

At Tabor the music is too slow, the children's ministry is too 1950s, and the people are unbelievably friendly.

And it's growing. Not like an uberchurch. But people are coming. Young couples, even. At a church of twenty regulars, one new family adds 20 percent. Hard for Willow to beat that percentage. Some of these are young professionals who have moved in to the Chicago area and are looking for church that reminds them of home—maybe even a home they never actually had. Tabor, with all its jagged edges, is it.

Some of that energy comes from the matriarch and patriarch couple of the church, who I'll call the Youngs.[2] They moved to the Chicago area from the West Coast as a young couple for his work, spent a lifetime in Illinois, and their kids and grandkids still attend and provide most of the leadership. When one of the Youngs preaches, it goes on too long. When they lead a youth event, it's never slick. Local advertisements, flyers paid for at great expense (for us anyway), featured several typos. But there all the members of that three-generation family were. Leading. The church is *theirs*, and their future is bound up with it, and vice versa. Where do we find that sort of commitment to *anything* in our age?

It astonishes me this sort of multigeneration family in one congregation is still possible, after cars and careers have scattered most of us from the dirt farms our ancestors once worked on. I have first cousins I wouldn't recognize on the street (one refused my friend request on Facebook once!). Here's a three-generation family, willing to invite you and me in on Sundays.

Some of Tabor's energy comes from Abe. Abe's been at Tabor forever. He still laments the wife he lost young, buried out back. Maybe she keeps him coming in a sense. He was at church every time we were, before we got there (and remember: we were the pastor's family). Abe passed out bulletins. He sang in the choir. He even lit the altar candles, as something of an overgrown acolyte. He usually had a prayer request. He didn't like to be in charge. Our predecessor, Pastor Charles, told us Abe approached him his very first Sunday. "I want to be an usher. But not head usher. That's too much responsibility, I just want to support the other ushers, not be head usher."

Charles looked on him and loved him. "Abe, we don't have head ushers. All we have is you."

Once, Abe got a new job that required him to be at work on Sundays. This didn't stop him. Tabor has a community of Filipino Methodists who worship on Sunday evenings. They do so in their native language, Tagalog. And Abe attended. One white guy in a sea of Asian Tagalog-speaking Methodists. "It's my church, and it's at a time I can come," he explained. "I can tell when they're saying the Lord's Prayer." And not much else.

Where do you find people like Abe outside the small church?

---

2. I have changed the names, locations, and identities of every person and church I speak of in this book except Jaylynn and me. I do want to talk about specific churches in specific places, since all ministry is specific and contextual. So I have scrambled and melded and composited identities.

Another man, Derrick, at Tabor, always responded the same way when I asked him how he was doing. "I'd be better if I had a job," he would say. It was brutally honest. Things would be better. No attempt to cover reality up. And he expected me to pray, which is why he kept telling me. Nowhere else in my life would I encounter a person without a job (this was before the financial meltdown in 2008, after which this is much more common, but the point remains). The only jobless people I'd see were downtown in Chicago with cups out for change. Derrick's wife worked, they were making the mortgage, but struggling, and every Sunday all that would be in the pew beside me. He prayed hard. Which made me pray harder.

That's why I thank God for the small church: Abe and Derrick and the Youngs. They belonged to me and me to them. When we were absent, they'd notice, and vice versa. Our stuff was in one another's faces, like Janet interrupting a sermon. Where do nonchurchgoers sit down beside jobless people? Where do people elsewhere in suburban Chicago come face to face with dogged, persistent loyalty to a single place like Abe's? Where do Chicago-area Yankees get country cool from northern California like the Youngs'? Where? Jesus spoke of the church as a vine and branches—he is the vine, we are the branches. We are linked to him insofar as we are linked to one another, and vice versa. Or to put it in the words of Peter Storey, the great Methodist anti-apartheid bishop from South Africa, "When Jesus was nailed to the cross, he nailed us to each other."[3]

This book is no fix-all. It's a bit more of a lament. I hope it's not a eulogy. Small churches are in trouble. These churches are pressed by their denominations to get big. Books on the small church are usually recipes for suicide. That is, they tell small churches how to get big, and how no longer to be small churches, which is like destroying a village in order to save it. This book's approach is different. It celebrates the small church as the primary way God has saved people through time, from the New Testament to now. Willow Creeks are an oddity, perhaps one God is also using, but a new thing.[4] They show up in the news disproportionately because they have a lot of people. But the old thing is Tabor. And with rising health insurance premiums, student loan debt for clergy, and the financial danger posed to small nonprofits generally, small churches are in real trouble. In a sense, this book is a prayer, praising God for the good of small churches, asking for help amidst this new trouble, and asking the rest of us to see their glory, which, God please not, may be passing away.

---

3. See Nathan Kirkpatrick's blog post at http://faithandleadership.com/blog/02-20-2009/nathan-kirkpatrick-the-christian-way-lay-someone.

4. William Lobdell, longtime religion reporter for the *LA Times*, told his editor there was a weekly gathering of 15,000 people in Orange County that the paper never covered. His editor refused to believe it. It was Saddleback Church. The editor told him to get busy covering it. These churches are a great thing, but they have plenty of defenders and admirers. Numbers make newsworthiness. But local churches, small and resilient and fragile as they are, are precious to a God whose eye is on a single sparrow.

Your Sins Are Forgiven

I've been puzzled previously by a moment in many communion liturgies. It's the confession of sin and assurance of pardon. The former makes sense—before approaching the Lord in bread and wine we should wash our hands, as it were, by confession. The assurance worries me a little. The minister confidently pronounces, "In the name of Jesus Christ, you are forgiven." How's *she* know? Have I confessed enough? Has everyone else here? Does it risk making forgiveness a perfunctory act and turning grace from something costly enough for a cross into something cheap?

But then the really puzzling part. The whole congregation replies, "In the name of Jesus Christ, *you* are forgiven." The way congregations I've served mumble that bit I'm not sure they're aware of the gravity of what they're saying. It makes sense for a minister to shower forgiveness on a church. Even we Protestants have some sort of intestinal memory of Catholic priests offering confession in a closed booth. We understand why a minister should perform a priestly function like that, even if, theologically, we might have problems with it, were it spelled out in detail. But if anything, this moment is bigger, more puzzling.

The whole congregation offers forgiveness to the minister. It's as if something enormously heavy needs lifting, and everybody together has to put their back into it. See that tree on that house? That car on top of that person? We gotta get it off. Or think of Jonah's companions on the boat, after they've figured out *his* God is the reason for the deadly storm. They don't ask his permission the second time they consider throwing him overboard. Altogether now, heave-ho!

"In the name of Jesus Christ, *you* are forgiven."

I only caught the gravity of it when a friend presided recently at chapel here at Duke Divinity School. She got the moment right. After she pronounced forgiveness on the congregation, and in anticipation of their collectively heaping forgiveness on her, she closed her eyes and bowed a little. That's all it took. She was a sinner, a "poor miserable wretch" in some of the church's older language, receiving an undeserved assurance of pardon from a body in unison. She wasn't even their pastor—it was a divinity school chapel service, what wrong could she have done to them? Yet in the gesture I saw it. A pastor needs that much forgiveness from that many people on a regular basis. It's argument enough for weekly communion.

"In the name of Jesus Christ, *you* are forgiven."

I know, theologically, it's not the congregation forgiving. It's not even the priestly minister who forgives them. It's an *assurance* of pardon after all. *God* does the pardoning. We sinners are just there to remind each other that (1) we are creatures in need of forgiveness and (2) we have a God who is eager to forgive, holding up fingers in a gesture of blessing that show, if we look carefully enough, the scarred hands that remind us how much it cost him. I worry that we don't take that moment seriously enough as a church. As we ministers pronounce that forgiveness it would be grace to feel a shiver, just an ounce of the pain it cost Jesus to offer it. It would keep us on our toes anyway.

But I worry even more that ministers don't notice the numerical shift in the middle of that assurance. Ministers can remind a congregation of God's forgiveness all by themselves. But it takes a whole congregation to forgive a pastor.

Especially one foisted on a small church with very little idea what he's doing.

CHAPTER TWO

A Little Growth Is Enough

W hy *small?*

What's the virtue in being a small church? In most denominations, and perhaps especially in the nondenominational Protestant world, bigger is better and biggest is best. We tell stories of places like Willow Creek and Saddleback with wide-eyed wonder. We send ministers to those places on a pilgrimage of sorts to learn how to replicate their success in Chicago and Orange County back home in Decorah or Siler City. Medieval pilgrims may have walked barefoot across northern Spain to see the tomb of St. James but we fly and pay through the nose to attend seminars to learn how to grow the ultimate prize: a big, influential, powerful church. Mainline imitators of these megaliths abound. See? It *can* be done.

I have no intention of disparaging large churches (though I reserve the right to tease them a little). They have their place in affluent suburbs with oceans of parking and people who expect their religion as convenient and prefab hip as their coffee. More benignly, large churches pay more than their fair share of the bills in our denominations, and often are gracious in teaching the rest of us. Excellent ministry often multiplies—more people want a good thing, who would wish to keep them away? I deeply admire the ministry of Adam Hamilton at the Church of the Resurrection in Kansas City with his 20,000 or so members. I love that Yoido Full Gospel Church in Seoul, South Korea, is pushing one million members, and is bigger than most cities in the world, let alone churches. Thousands of people are thousands of individual souls, precious to God, deserving of the best we can offer in ministry.

But big churches can take care of themselves. The problem is with denominational officials and pastors and laypeople who think their small church should be big and are made to (or make themselves), feel like failures when it doesn't happen.

I arrived at Beech Grove United Methodist Church in Zebulon County, North Carolina, in the summer of 2002 to apologies for how small they were. "We used to have more people," one lady said, leaving the sentence dangling, as though unsure of where the multitude went. It was hard to believe they once had. The church has seven or eight pews on each side, with another three on each side tucked in the back in little enclaves that must have once been separable Sunday school rooms (*someone* thought they didn't need any more room in the sanctuary—until someone else made those separable rooms into a sort of permanent balcony on the same level as the rest of the church). We could seat eighty or so comfortably. Many more for a funeral or special event and things started to get call-the-fire-marshal snug. And we were mostly full already—forty was a bad Sunday, sixty a good one.

What made her think her church was a failure for being small?

Maybe it was the fact that many of Beech Grove's former members had left for a big Baptist church in Danville, the largest nearby city. Not much is big in Danville. Jaylynn and I liked exercising at Dan Daniel Memorial Park in Danville (most things are, in fact, named for Dan there). Martin Luther King, Jr.'s visit to Danville in the 1960s brought about beatings so savage that images of bloodied marchers were beamed around the world. Goodyear and a tobacco company kept people employed. Old-timers told me that in their childhood Danville also had 40,000 residents, same as Greensboro, North Carolina. Then North Carolina's governor helped JFK carry the Tar Heel State. He became Transportation Secretary, and north-south I-85 took a little east-west detour across the length of North Carolina. Greensboro is pushing a quarter million residents now. Danville: 40,000. Still.

But every place in the South has big churches, and Danville had its requisite big Baptist church with a charismatic preacher and adoring multitudes. One member of Beech Grove told me she'd seen him ride his motorcycle out onto the church stage one Sunday. This thrilled her.

She told me as I visited inside her modest home. Its wood-paneled walls and well-stained floor suggested she did her own cleaning and didn't mind giving herself a day off. It could have used a grandchild or even an adult kid to waft through and lighten things up. The musty smell suggested windows and doors hadn't been opened in a while. She was neither poor nor rich. Just surviving.

Somehow, though, her cheerful spirit was infectious. She laughed as soon as she told stories of economic hardship—stuff not paid for. Her face was as bright as her trinketry. She was a happy, upbeat person. Or at least she was trying to be. And Community Baptist Church (or was it Dan Daniel Baptist in Danville?) was happy and upbeat and perfect for her.

She called me her "visiting pastor" and Pastor Motorcycle her "preaching pastor." I needn't have asked whether he ever visited her house or who would have done the funeral for her mother if asked. I thought if I visited her regularly she'd realize how badly we needed her and come back to Beech Grove, where they'd notice if she were gone, not feeling good, or singing like Jesus had come back. But she never did. Maybe I should've been clearer how badly we wanted her to. She probably thought church was about her needs only, instead of the needs of a communal body. And that small body in Zebulon needed her much more than Community did.

Several of my older people had lost their children to Community. They'd had children of their own, and Beech Grove just couldn't compete with the kids programming at Community. So my older people lost their grandchildren on Sunday morning too. These had been replaced by other middle-aged people with their own small children, but it wasn't the same. When the children of the church would reappear once or twice a year at Homecoming or Christmas, their parents looked happier than I ever saw them otherwise. I remember one such high holy day with my parishioner with the wonderful name of Roscoe and his five children and their spouses and kids, dressed to the nines, in the front two pews where no one ever sat, ready to hear God's word from me that day. No idea what I said. Didn't matter.

I'm sure Community did something well, or else people wouldn't go there. Big churches thrive when they subdivide into smaller units, so that someone knows everyone by name. They don't just gather anonymously. Even then there are problems. The sociologist Mark Chaves tells of a megachurch pastor who admitted to him he didn't even know the names of everyone on his *staff*. Now, what sort of reflection is this of a shepherd who knows the sheep by name, who lays his life down for them? I've pastored people with wonderful names like Roscoe, Abe, Ophelia, Josiah, Eldridge, Lula, Bright, Keturah, Leonidas. Each name thrills with memories of prayer, time together, shared grace. This guy not knowing his staff's names isn't just bad form. It's not the gospel.

I never visited Community. Maybe I should've gone to see the wave of the future. No doubt my denominational execs looking at the bad news of bottom lines would have wished us to be a bit more like it. Suggestions around church were often punctuated with "And if we did that, we could get some more people." That would have been the real prize. They almost looked over their shoulder at their kids and grandkids at Community as they said it. What was left unspoken: if we can't get our own children, how on earth do we get anybody else's?

The thing is, we were financially healthy, meeting our $80,000 budget while I was there, and beginning work on a $180,000 parsonage. They burned the note four years after we broke ground. They *did* have children and middle-aged people, just not with the same last names as the old-timers, the Landers, Clintons, and McGowans (pronounced MACKgown). We even grew a little— a family a year for two years, four new people each time. With eighty people, four new ones a year is not bad—5 percent per year actually, 10 percent growth total in my two years. Even with these signs of health, there was a general air of resignation to failure about the place for not being huge. There in Zebulon County of all places! Where did they expect the multitudes to come from?

This strikes me as the right sort of growth. Not a gushing torrent. But not a dry, rusty faucet either. Denominational officials see too much of the latter. Pastors hear too much insistence on the former. Let us agree there should be growth, enough to keep things fresh—to add an official graft of living tissue onto the wounded places of the body of Christ. But not so much that we can't learn new people's *names*—let alone let them into our life enough to question whether we're being as holy as our baptism calls us to be.

My first sermon at Beech Grove was about the God of small things. There are famous stories that lend to our infatuation with numbers—the parable of the talents with its tenfold return, Peter's preaching in Acts that draws thousands. But other stories point the other direction—Jesus says we only need two or three for worship, the gospel is the smallest of seeds, the gift of even a cup of cold water to a child will not go unrewarded. Acts gives us no sigh of resignation when Paul's preaching in Athens only brings two converts. In fact, it dutifully records their names: "Dionysius the Areopagite and a woman named Damaris" (Acts 17:34). God chose Israel not because she was the biggest or best—if God had, everyone would have expected it. *Of course* run-of-the-mill deities prefer the Babylonians. But not the biblical God. And arguably the thrust of the New Testament is not toward the megachurch like Community but toward the precious nature of every single thing God has created, with human beings as creation's crown. "The goal here," one wise leader at Beech Grove said as we debated church growth, "is to bring one soul to Jesus." One soul, just one, and it's like you've saved the whole world.

So this book is a celebration of the small church. Lots of books about the small church amount to "how to make your small church big." Community Baptist up the road is the model. A certain high-powered megachurch in our denomination spins its mythology this way: the pastor set his mind on pastoring a large church. Never mind that his wasn't one for years and years. He planned like it was, acted like it was, saw what it would be before it was. And then it was. People came, buildings were built, international missions launched, money poured in. And then the kingdom of God came. Or not. Anyway, do the math. He's sold thousands of books, more registrations to conferences, all offering the recipe for how to imitate him. How many purchasers of those products have successfully gone and done likewise? Very, very few. It reminds me of Walker Percy's image of a man on a train reading a book about positive thinking. He saw the man furl his brow, shake his head, and sadly close the book. He thought to himself there was no better way to make suicide desirable than to read such books. So too with the make-your-church-big literature. Once in a blue moon it works. Mostly it makes ministers and churches feel miserable. Very little of it has anything to do with Jesus.

We Methodists do small well. Perhaps too well. It's been alleged, with some justice, that our system is rigged to *keep* churches small, or at least to make life unduly difficult for large ones. The vast majority of our churches are still of the small rural type, perhaps because we do well at staffing those churches through our use of "multipoint charges." My wife pastored two of these appointments. She was pastor at Buelah and Rehobeth churches in Zebulon County on her two-point charge. On a special occasion like one church's homecoming, the other would cancel and everybody would worship at the one place. These two were friendly enough that they could alternate who went early and who went late— in some other settings, the bigger or wealthier church chooses its time and the other one sucks it up. They didn't have to announce on the Web site or the church signs which was meeting when. If you were coming you already knew.

Buelah and Rehobeth were once a decent horse ride apart, and two points on a five-point charge back in the day. The church growth literature would say to close 'em. Merge 'em. Make 'em one big church with some prayer of a future. The default argument against such a move is each church has its own cemetery. Usually this is derided as bad logic. But as far as I'm concerned, that's reason enough. Christianity is a matter of keeping faith with the dead. The cemetery argument leaves implicit a more substantial claim: each church has more than 200 years of history baptizing and communing and sinning and forgiving on that very spot. And you'd want to close them for expedience's sake? To enhance possibilities for church growth based on what some guy in California wrote in his book? Jesus says, "If any of you put a stumbling block before one of these little ones who believe in me, it would be better for you if a great millstone were hung around your neck and you were thrown into the sea" (Mark 9:42).

CHAPTER THREE

Priestly People

Jaylynn's two churches had a bit less verve than mine at Beech Grove, it's safe to say. Both were "family chapels" of a sort, so named because one or two dominant families runs and pays for each. Both were filled with first citizens of the county: teachers, lawyers, local politicians, retired people with means. Zebulon might be one of the poorer counties in North Carolina but we didn't see it, except around the edges. These folks became our friends—watching sports with us, celebrating our baby's birth, overlooking our faults, taking care of our home, bringing food by the barrelful when we needed it, loving us. And we knew them by name. And some of their cousins by name. Like God knows us.

Rehobeth tells the story of their founding at their annual Homecoming—an anniversary celebration of sorts, on the Sunday closest to the day the church was founded. That was in 1770 for Rehobeth. Yes, the church is older than the Republic she's in. A few folks from the county went down to a revival with Francis Asbury in Hillsborough and got saved. They came back up and gathered for worship under a big old oak tree in the community. When that tree became a stump, the preacher would still fire away from up there, exhorting sinners to be saved and saints to be sanctified. Then they'd spread out and eat. They weren't always first citizens—a stone in the graveyard says simply, "George's mama." They must've had their problems in those days too. Think of what they've been through: war and peace, secession and reconstruction, epidemics, poverty, and then the wealth of *some* parts of the New South. It's lovely isn't it?—to imagine a few converts trying to make more converts in this rural farming community for more years than the United States has existed.

The patriarch there is a man named Leonidas Johnston. He is the original barrel-chested big bear of a man. He'd shake your hand and you'd be glad to have it back. He talked in clipped sentences, like when he said his name, it sounded more like "Lee Jnns," said with a sort of friendly snarl. His glasses were thick and his step slow, like he owned the place, and he about did. His several daughters were leading members and married others, his one son was another, and they invited us in to their lives straightaway. He was all the more lovely for being a widower, and perhaps because he was alone his children looked after him more regularly. But we didn't know what a kind heart he had, and were put off by our first impression. We were afraid Leon might be our chief antagonist. "They're like alligators," one pastor told me. "There's one in every pond."

During our first week there Jaylynn proposed something new. Not anything radical, but something that would require others to be on board. "I got to run that by Leon," one leader told her. "Because nobody f**ks with Leon."

What did he just say?

It wasn't a bad description of things. Even if, for a moment, it confirmed our worst fears. But Leon turned out to be our closest companion. "We love you," he'd openly tell Jaylynn. "And your family. Come over anytime." And we did. His politics were Paleolithic—when a lawyer-member told us they closed the old county prison because it was considered too punitive he spewed, "Can't make it bad enough far as I'm concerned." But when he heard we were pregnant he left the sweetest voice mail message we've ever heard. "Jlyn, Json [he wasn't big on vowels], just herd! Congrtchlations! This is gret! We love yuh! So proud uh yuh! Yuh dun good!" Why can't they all be like Leon?

Buelah was a quieter bunch. They had a monthly breakfast for the men in the community, for which my sedan would be the only non-pickup in the lot. We'd scarf down biscuits and bacon amidst grunts about golf and NASCAR. One guy there was pushing not 300, but 400 pounds. One holler about bacon being out drew this bellow from him, "That's a terrible thing to tell a fat man!" There were no illusions.

Jaylynn proposed that Buelah clean house one time. A few old ladies came over that Sa'erdey, as they'd call it. I was worried we'd be at it for weeks. But those women could work! "Let me carry that," I'd plead. "No, no, this is nothing," and a bag of trash the size of me would go flying past. Who was the seventy-year-old and who the thirty-year-old again? Something about having begun working hard in tobacco fields as little girls, I guess. I had no idea just how unused the unused church library was until I came across an Easter egg so far past rotten it didn't smell anymore. It was glued to an activity bulletin that had the date on it, "Easter 1958."

A few hours' work and that room was Jaylynn's office, complete with a new computer, seats for counseling, a view of the rolling green yard, and a new day. Buelah was, and is, a gorgeous church, bright white inside with brilliant red and dark wood ornamentation, golden lamps and oodles of sunshine pouring through the windows. It just needed a bit of TLC, for which its first female minister in memory was the perfect person. And some old women, who worked us kids to shame.

Buelah and Rehobeth together were responsible for our pastor's house, still called by the wonderfully antiquated name of "parsonage" (never mind that no one called us "parsons"). This was the primary problem with a multipoint charge. If Jaylynn wanted a new washing machine, she had to meet with not one, but two committees to bring the thing about.

She would have conversations like this: "So we need a new washing machine."

"Why? My husband and I gave the church that one not too long ago."

"That was a thoughtful gift at the time, years ago now. And it's spewing oil on our clothes, ruining them."

"Well, there was a day when pastors didn't mind washing clothes by hand."

"Yeah, there was" (thought to self: *why did I skip out on law school?*).

We thought we figured out a way to save some money one time though. We'd just leave the AC off. Sure, this was North Carolina in the summer, but we were young and tough. Until one of our older members came over with a pie. We greeted her, all sat down, and she looked around, "What's wrong with the air conditionin'?" She remembered—the Old South didn't become the new south until AC hit. Atlanta and Charlotte don't fill with Yankees without it. We might have seminary debt to pay off, but this was ridiculous.

This same lady after 9/11 called my wife, her pastor, to tell her how stressed out she was. As though Osama was going to hit tower one, then tower two, then sweet Esther's house in Zebulon County. We told her to cut the TV off.

Our first week, there a man as big and solid as a tree trunk who came and knocked on our door. Jeremiah Dickerson was still in his waders from hunting. After he knocked he'd stood far away from the door, like he was afraid we'd smell him. He hunted more than he came to church. And his accent made even Zebulon Countyers turn their heads. "I got 'bout a hundred acres a tabacca down a ways. Y'all come see me if you got 'ny problems." Jeremiah would often find arrowheads in those fields and give them to his grandchildren and others in church.

Jerry, as we came to call him, had done two tours in Korea. He'd had wild days behind him others knew about and refrained from discussing. Jerry would only talk about his salvation. "You get your life back right with God, get back on the straight 'n narrow, you got a lot to be thankful for."

Jaylynn went out to the mailbox one morning just down the hill from the parsonage, still disheveled, hoping not to be seen by anybody. Naturally Jerry pulled up. "What has you up so early?" He asked her in his booming voice, which would have been a baritone if he ever much sang. "I've got to take our new dog to the vet to get him neutered," she announced, happy it was someone we were glad to see. Jerry stared at her. "You go to the doctor for that? Let's take 'em back to the house, get some rubber bands, I'll do it for you."

Now it was her turn to stare.

"Uh, no thanks, Jerry, see you in church Sunday."

"Alright," he smiled, aware of and bemused by our differences more even than we were.

Now don't let my description of Jerry make you think he's not smart. You have to be smart to farm nowadays. It takes computers and chemicals and Spanish and all sorts of knowledge his granddaddy didn't need. Jerry also ran political campaigns for local officials that rivaled high-paying consultant gigs. And he talked like his people long had, and was as loyal as they ever were. It's odd that Southernness still means "stupid" in American academe and places like Manhattan. I once heard the novelist Reynolds Price say once that if you take the South out of American letters, you're left with a big white fish.

Jerry asked me once to do two things before I left the county: to work a day in the tobacco fields and to go bear hunting with him. Tobacco is disgusting work. The narcotic is a natural insecticide, and those who work in it know it's poison. They have to shower after they touch it, it sticks to their body and can make them sick. Hispanic immigration has its own particulars everywhere, but in tobacco country its cause is largely that nobody, black or white, wants to work in the tobacco fields anymore, no matter what their daddy did for money. Kids used to spend their summers in the field, now they spend them like every other American kid: in front of video games. I took a pass on that one.

The hunting offer I accepted. "OK, Jerry, let's go," I said. "OK, we go for two weeks." *Two weeks*?! I'm not going into the woods for two weeks with guns with you! He took it graciously. Bear hunting is best done on the North Carolina coast, not the mountains, since the swamps keep people away and bears don't like people. Still, it takes a while to find a bear to shoot at. Hence the large time commitment. Maybe it was the Korean War in him, but Jerry liked to hunt things that could kill you back. I suggested we start with something less fearsome, like, say, little fluffy bunnies, and only slowly work our way up to, say, dragons. His entry in the church cookbook was for bear stew. Its directions? (1) get a 150 lb. bear; (2) chop it into bite-sized bits. OK, I'll run down to Walmart and pick me up one of those. . . . But he was serious. Brought a slow cooker full of it to church one time. It was spicy, gamey, and *good*.

Not long after we left we got the saddest letter we ever got, worse almost than hearing somebody died. Jerry wrote to say they were taking away his guns. Before Korea, before conversion, before the current healthy marriage, there had been problems. We still don't know what, but the law did. Legislature had passed a bill saying if you'd done time for a felony you couldn't get a hunting license. It'd have been more humane to take a major organ from Jerry. He was inconsolable. He asked us to write "hizzoner" to ask for a pardon, but everyone knows how forthcoming those are these days.

Once, coming back from a mission trip to Russia (itself a story—see below), we thought we had arrangements for Jerry to pick us up at the airport. We'd been traveling for days from Eastern Europe, were exhausted, and found no truck waiting for us. I barked an angrier-than-I-ought message into Jerry's answering machine. Apparently he had to pass the duty off to someone else, but underestimated the other man's hardness of hearing, so no one came. "Jason, I got this message about no one being there and all. I'm so sorry." Now I was sorry, this man who'd killed other men and bears and, with Jesus' help, his own sin, felt my rebuke for letting him down. "Jerry, I'm sorry. I'd trust my life with you." He paused. I wondered if he'd accept my apology (and why again was I apologizing when he'd failed to show up? Southern hospitality will do strange things to you). "Well, if you trusted me with your life, it'd be in good hands."

Our life was in good hands those years, hands like Jerry's. It could have gone otherwise. We'd both been taught in seminary about the sinful nature of things like violence, racism, classism, sexism, whatever other sort of -ism. Jerry embodied most of those, or had in his past (and, really, among us white southern males, who doesn't?). It'd have been easy to be at odds with him, just looking at the syllabi in our courses. Once, during prayer requests, when I was subbing for Jaylynn (a time-honored pastor spouse's role), he asked prayers of thanks "for those dying for our freedom in Iraq."

I'll maintain that the gospel is one of peace, of God's breaking of himself on the cross to end our violence, of the drowning of differences of race and gender in the waters of baptism (Gal 3:28). We preached as much often—hence Jerry's challenge during prayer requests. The best sermon I've ever heard preached was Jaylynn's the week after 9/11. The text was Romans 5, where Paul marvels that Christ dies *for sinners*. It makes some sense to die for a good person, we can understand this sort of sacrifice. "But God proves his love for us in that while we still were sinners Christ died for us" (Rom 5:8). She choked up as she proclaimed to them, "God dies for murderers." She didn't even have to say "Osama bin Laden." They got it. On his way out, Denny Ray said to her, "That was a little bit different slant than Billy Graham had."

But on other occasions they weren't so eager to hear the nonviolence business. When Jerry asked for that prayer request, eyes met mine coolly—not angrily, but certainly curious what I'd say, maybe even dubious whether I'd do the right thing. Good thing the liturgy *tells* you what to say, and doesn't make you make it up on the fly. I said what one says at that moment: "Lord, in your mercy, *hear our prayer.*"

If there were a contest for the extravagance of one's love for other people, Jerry would win hands down; if this life were a race for holiness in which those who run hardest win the prize, as some scripture suggests (1 Cor 9:24-27), then Jerry wins hands down. Only he'd have slowed down, long since, to pick up stragglers like us, and carry them over, in his bear-claw mitts.

I tell these stories of particular people because particular people are God's means to save us. The small church is God's best means to save us because God doesn't save in general. Let me explain what I mean.

The first stories of God's saving work are directed to humanity in general. Adam and Eve—all of our forbearers—are given a charge. They fail. Just a few chapters later God grows tired of humanity's wickedness and wipes out the whole lot, except for one justice-loving family (which has its own warts, as it turns out). Then shortly after, God chooses one man: Abram. "Go from your country and your kindred and your father's house to the land that I will show you. I will make of you a great nation, and I will bless you, and make your name great, so that you will be a blessing. . . . In you all the families of the earth shall be blessed" (Gen 12:1-3). God saves through a particular, elect people, Israel. We Christians believe we're the fruit of Genesis 12:3—in Abram-turned-Abraham, all the world, including us Gentiles, are also blessed.

Modern Christianity has often been embarrassed by this particularity. We prefer a God who saves in general, who is close to all, accessible to all, equally loving of all, all all all. That's fine. It's true too. God does reach all of us sinners with the grace of Jesus, as Romans and other books make clear. Yet God starts with the particular—Adam, Noah, Abram, Israel. And God stays with the particular even as he reaches to the rest of us: church, sacraments, bread, wine, one another. If God's presence is not rooted in these quite physical and particular means of grace, eventually we will lose a sense of God's presence anywhere.

So it's important that Paul and others name particular people in their churches. "May the Lord grant mercy to the household of Onesiphorus . . . when he arrived in Rome, he eagerly searched for me and found me—may the Lord grant that he will find mercy from the Lord on that day!" (2 Tim 1:16-18). Just as Onesiphorus barreled through the streets of Rome searching for the apostle, the Lord will barrel through all obstacles and find Onesiphorus with mercy at the judgment. Salvation here comes to particular people with names. This is the way God has always worked.

So too God works through particular people now. We can hide from this theological truth by staying at home and watching church on TV, or attending a show of a big church where we don't have to do business with any actual breathing human beside us. But the small church won't let us stay anonymous. It mediates grace to us through particular people—beautiful, flawed, graced people like Jerry, who seek mercy with us from the Lord on that day for the sake of the rest of our days.

The small church may just be Jesus' means of liberating us from the anonymity and the accursed loneliness of life in our world. If we just stick with it.

Grief from Pastors; Grace from Parishioners

We almost didn't get the two-point charge in Zebulon County. We almost got the two-point charge in Pearlsburg, Virginia. That one made Zebulon seem downright cosmopolitan. The house was down in a ditch from the road. There was a parsonage dog attached to the parsonage. Nobody knew where it came from or whose it was, but it was part of the deal. Mange and all, we had to care for it. The dishwasher hung out in the middle of the kitchen, with no crevice to put it in, like a permanent place to stub your toe (and most of the rest of you) at night in the dark, with nowhere to remove it to. The basements of the churches smelled mustier than, well, most church basements. Jaylynn would've been their first female pastor. This would've been fine. Expected really, from our vantage. What was unexpected was that the district superintendent ("DS" in Methodist parlance, a group of whom is above the preacher and below the bishop and tries to mediate between the two) wanted to leave me in the car while introducing her to her new church. "If we all walk in and they see that you're the man, they'll assume you're the pastor," she said, apparently knowing of what she spoke as a woman pastor. OK, I'll wait. So Jaylynn met her first charge with me sitting shotgun of the DS's car outside, listening to Garth Brooks. For what seemed like forever. Why was I not with my wife for one of the most important moments in her career, her life even?

Finally I decided this was ridiculous, and came in. The DS glared at me. As soon as she could say "This is Jaylynn" she hastened to add "your new pastor."

All the cloak-and-dagger nonsense aside, the church members seemed fine with the female pastor (it was the female DS who seemed agitated over it all).

"Let's go around and introduce ourselves and say how we each serve in the church," the DS said, harmlessly enough. "I come from a large family that lived by the sea," she started. "We fished for fish one season and crabs the next. My mama ran a beauty parlor that twirled my hair up real high like this. . . ." She went on. For another ten minutes. We looked around at the other fifteen people who were to introduce themselves and did the math. Suddenly the first-female-preacher thing didn't seem like such a big deal.

Next was Lois. "I'm Lois, I been at this church forty years, I serve on this committee."

Silence.

DS: "Is that all, Lois?"

"Why, yes."

"You don't do anything more at this church than serve on this committee?"

"It's a lot of work. I'm real busy."

"Uh huh. Next?"

Why does the church put up with its leadership? Why did those laypeople put up with us pastors and DSs? We infiltrate their communities, barely understand them, speak down to them, literally, from that pulpit. DSs send crummy preachers or else take away good ones to bigger churches first chance they get. And yet when they show up they're treated with respect bordering on reverence. Lois should have bawled that woman out, and had every right to. Instead they bear with us.

Maybe there is a God.

Zebulon came along unexpectedly. They had a last-second retirement. Pastor Jacobs had stored up weeks of vacation without telling anybody. Now he was gone. He wasn't waiting until annual conference, when Methodist ministers all swap on Moving Day, he was just gone in January. "He figured he had six months' vacation stored up; he never took a vacation day while he was here," one member told us. The DS muttered, "I don't remember anyone ever storing up vacation time in our church before. And I'm sure it's not in the *Discipline*." Another layperson said, "Funny, I don't remember him working much when he was here!" When we opened a phone bill to see if we owed a portion of it, since our move didn't coincide perfectly with AT&T's billing schedule, we sent it to Reverend Jacobs and got a furious note back. "I have never once not paid my bills on time!" As if we were bill collectors. Sorry, dude, chill out, mail 'em a check. It's a marvel Methodist ministers speak to one another at all.

Buelah-Rehobeth would pay a bit more than Pearlsburg, a few grand, which was a lot for us. We felt bad making a decision based on money, so we called around to other minister friends to ask what we should do. Surely it'd be the virtuous thing to take the job with less money. That's what Jesus would want—have you *seen* what he says about money in the Gospels? And surely we should live in the town we liked less, right? We sacrifice, Jesus rewards us, that's how it works, isn't it?

We called a mentor of ours to ask what he thought. His wife answered. This might even be better. She was a pastor's spouse, daughter of a pastor, grand-daughter of another. She'd set us right.

"Let me get this straight. You're hesitating not to take that job *because* it's more money?"

"Yeah. Isn't that what we were taught we should do in seminary? Doesn't less money mean more faithfulness?"

"Why's that again?"

"Well, it's not very much like Jesus is it?"

Pause.

"You'd be crazy not to take that job. *Crazy*. You hear me? *Crazy!*" All the pathos of a pastor's wife, a pastor's daughter and granddaughter spilled out. "You'll make less money your whole career! You'll have to wait another appoint-ment just to move up to an appointment that's as high paying as the one you'd be turning down! Do you want to be like my grandmother who tried to dry dia-pers in a parsonage without heat and had them freeze on the line, *do you?!*"

We mentioned another older pastor whom we'd admired. We'd imagined ask-ing him—what would Pastor Samuel do? "What would Jesus do" is entirely too ephemeral—it has no connection to our actual lives. It does very little good to try to choose which car to buy with that bracelet slogan. It suggests Jesus' *absence*—as though we have to conjure his spirit for a new day. But Christ is alive, risen, going before us, present in his saints. It makes perfect sense to ask what a saint like Pastor Samuel would do—for in such a one Jesus is presently working.

But our interlocutor would have none of it. "What? Have you *seen* his beach house?"

Apparently even a saint, or at least this one, doesn't simply give everything away.

That settled that. And it taught us something important. We had a sort of noblesse oblige approach to salary and our own happiness as a family. Surely Jesus wants us to be unhappy, we said, in effect—what else could he mean by asking us to take up our crosses? But another swath of the gospel was missing. Surely Jesus also wants us to thrive, to live life abundantly, to practice ministry in ways that brought us joy and so enabled others to find joy through our ministry. God's people occasionally do wind up martyrs, or bearing significant crosses through life in their ministries. We would do some of that. But the ancient church *dis-couraged* people from seeking out martyrdom when they could avoid it. It does no one any good to seek to be slightly less happy for Jesus' sake. Others will do that ministry joyfully. Not you.

So, just married, we packed the moving truck ourselves and set out for Zebulon County. The parsonage wasn't much then, if it ever had been. But the house was a miracle in the eyes of such as us who were used to apartment life. Three bedrooms, wood floors, great exterior windows, basement with an office we called the PE teacher's office (steel cabinets, bad fluorescent lighting, just like back in elementary school), more room than we knew what to do with. How would we fill it all?

Obviously not with church people's help.

We'd heard if you moved cheaply you could pocket the difference. Just starting out as a family, this would've been a real help. Except apparently the conference had changed that policy. They just hadn't told us newbies. There was no incentive now not to hire the World's Most Expensive Movers and pay them lavishly. We showed up with a moving truck expecting an army of volunteers to help us move in. There was no one. We couldn't even get the door open. We'd heard wrong.

Eventually some church people showed up with flowers. The ladies were slightly more dressed up than usual to meet the new pastor's family. They hadn't planned anything more strenuous than a cup of tea and the livening-up of our first flower arrangement. We rolled our eyes, and went back to chuffing over overstuffed boxes. Finally one woman girded up her loins and feigned enthusiasm, "Come on ladies," and they soldiered some boxes into the house. Our fairly pitiful distress brought out their readiness to help—how could it not? One called her husband who took the top off my desk with a screwdriver and to get it in the house and dragged it in on a blanket (it stayed when we moved—no one could ever figure out how to get it back out). Others moved boxes, food, pictures. We were in. We had a house. A life.

In one way Methodists serve rural communities like this well. We send seminary-trained pastors and spare local churches long searches for a new minister. We keep such churches open longer than some other denominations would, and give them more stability than many nondenominational or independent outfits have. It's hard to imagine how an independent congregation of some sort could have found Jaylynn and me, credentialed us, sent us to a place like Zebulon, and paid us enough to stay there more than a few minutes. We speak of being a "connectional" church—not independent agents. That connection made all this possible.

Yet I wonder whether such churches don't do the lion's share of the work in our communion. We showed up, barely sure how to be married, and with no clue how to live in a community like theirs. And they moved our stuff in when they didn't have to (in fact, it was their money going to the conference we should have been using to hire movers! Who should've given us the memo on that?!). They gave us a "pounding," which I hadn't heard of, but am glad now I have. It's not a beating up, but a pound of this, a pound of that, sugar and flour and all (which we weren't even sure what to do with). They bore sermons they should never have had inflicted on them, and when we preached well they acted like the proudest grandparents of a baby who just pooped in the right place. And when we seasoned up, several years in, we were gone. By then we had a second kid coming, needed more money, and were ready for a place with some more entertainment and better schools. They knew it would happen, it happens with their own children, and they didn't begrudge it a bit.

The town where we lived was actually called Branch. We called the parsonage the Branch Ranch. It had a fake rock covering up the well in the front. This was important to know. I didn't at first.

"Why am I not getting a water bill?" I asked one man. He fell out laughing.

A friend from the city asked us why the rock looked so fake, when in the theater they make real-looking fake rocks all the time. I liked her response more.

Our nearest neighbors were a country mile away. We could see them clearly enough, there at the top of the next hill. The hills roll gently there, so that animals stretching in the sunlight made silhouettes on adjoining hills. Whoever owned the hay field surrounding our house cut it a few times a year, then left the hay bails to rot. They'd have kept Monet busy. It looked like a driving range behind our house. A professional golfer could hit balls that would pose no danger to passersby, for there were none. We heard warnings of wild hogs out in the woods back that way. But we never saw any. Just bounding deer and rotting hay.

A DS in Illinois told me once he placed a city girl in a country appointment. She called the first night. "It's too loud here," she complained, "I can't sleep."

"Loud? What do you mean?"

"I hear cows, owls, bugs, coyotes. Things are alive outside my window."

She was used to elevated trains and car horns and crazy people screaming, but the screech owl was another thing entirely.

That was us, at the Branch Ranch. It was noisy, in the best sort of quiet way.

I remember a three-piece-suited man standing up before a gathering of a few dozen of us ministers to explain why there was no reason we couldn't retire as millionaires. Now we were talking! He was going to show us how, through our church's successful pension program. Our eyes got big. We were in a church for this meeting—if he'd have held an altar call we'd have all gone forward and accepted the three-piece-suited man into our hearts as our Lord and Savior. It seems preposterous now, I know, after the stock market meltdown of 2008. But at the time it was salve for our ears.

The small church teaches a different way with money, provision, ambition. It's a place where you can make enough, if you're frugal. You can't get rich there, and you shouldn't starve. You'll make more than most people in the community, but not near as much as some. But it's enough. An abundance really, over which one can thank God. One friend of mine, committed to the rural church, has promised himself to stay at our church's minimum salary his whole career. He'd better demonstrate some incompetence if he expects them to leave him there.

It's about right to make enough, but not too much. St. Paul wrote to the Corinthians, quoting Exodus, that "the one who had much did not have too much, / and the one who had little did not have too little" (2 Cor 8:15). Even more poignantly, Paul thanks the Philippians for their support of his ministry, "a fragrant offering, a sacrifice acceptable and pleasing to God" (Phil 4:18). I remember a smart undergraduate at Duke, a skeptic of religion, talking about watching the plate go by at his church. "That was the exploitation of religion, right there." I take his point—either my ministerial faithfulness made their giving a gift, or my laziness would mean I was essentially on the take. Either way, I made one-fifth of what he did in his first job in finance.

We live in a world of unparalleled separation between rich and poor, in which the rich have more than ever, and the poor, well, as little as the poor have always had. As ministers, we all have master's degrees, and some of us have doctoral degrees, the works. And we will make much less money than people in most other professions with masters or doctoral degrees. And it will sting at times— just wait for that postcard about the private jaunt to Jamaica in your friend's own plane.

And just so, perhaps, we're a witness to the world that it's important not to have too little, and not to have too much. And if we're lucky, or blessed, our desire might even come in-line with this reality. Is it too much to ask for a grace that big?

CHAPTER FIVE

Faces Shining

Being a preacher's husband is the best job on planet earth. Like preachers' wives you're expected to sit there and gaze adoringly at your spouse, to laugh at the jokes, nod slowly and sagaciously at the profound stuff, stand by her side as she shakes hands at the end of the day, and be her mental and spiritual support. Occasionally you step in and take prayer requests or preach. But when you do so you'd better be ready to be less impressive than her. In our case that wasn't hard. King James translated Genesis 2:20, which comes off in the NRSV: "For the man there was not found a *helper* as his partner," as "help-meet" (italics added). That was me, a help-meet, only with chest hair.

Being a male help-meet is great. You aren't expected to bake. Or attend teas. Or the United Methodist Women's meetings. As our teacher Stanley Hauerwas, the gruff-speaking theologian from Texas, says of being a pastor's husband himself, "I'm hell at the bishop's tea." People don't gossip about your clothes or make comments about your homemaking. You're a dude, they know that's not part of being a pastor's husband. Whatever pastor's husbands are supposed to do, laypeople haven't figured it out yet. One pastor's-husband friend of mine, with long hair in back and a balding pate up front, was approached by a similarly visaged man one weeknight at his church. "Dude, man, AA meeting's this way."

Pastor's wives don't get this sort of unsolicited directional advice.

Buelah and Rehobeth taught me the theological importance of a compassionate pastor's spouse. Jaylynn was often frazzled after preaching, especially when she had to hop in the car, speed to the next church, and preach the whole thing over again. She had little memory power left to catch who was sick, who was in town, who had something to celebrate, who just looked a little off and distant that morning. Once I started pastoring on my own I made a rule: don't tell me anything Sunday morning that you expect me to remember. But while I was still her pastoral help-meet, I had plenty of time and space to take notes for her, precisely when she had no such luxury.

So I was her memory for her.

And this was easy to be, for people were there ready to tell the things in their lives that needed pastoral salve. They'd figure telling me was as good as telling her, maybe better. I had time she didn't have, running around to get service ready, to look them in the eye, ask them how they were doing, ask a more probing follow-up question if their answer didn't seem right. The pressure was off for me as the help-meet. I wasn't technically the pastor, I just had to ferret out the problem, not the answer. We'd get home and I'd run down everything I had, which would then fill her pastoral calendar that week. It was true what the older ministers said, however patronizing it sounded to my ears, that pastors' wives ran the church. Here I was, pastor's husband, and similarly indispensable. I just didn't look as good doing it.

What we didn't do, that we should have, was pray over these requests together. That most important pastoral function, of standing as a priest before God on behalf of the people, we let slip. Why? We prayed on our own, for sure. We prayed together for our own family quarrels and issues. We prayed when we visited others' churches on vacation and when we were in real trouble, hands held, usually in a car, amidst tears. We're not averse to prayer. But we didn't pray like we ought to have for our own churches. Looking back that may be our biggest omission. I've heard of one pastor who keeps Christmas cards from everyone she gets them from, and at dinner the rest of the year they take one and pray for that family. Jaylynn had a prie-dieu installed in her office to offer up entreaty to God. I'm not saying we did none of it. But we didn't do enough. What if we made a regular nightly practice of approaching God on behalf of God's people gathered at Zebulon County?

It might serve no obvious use. It's not like heart ailments or broken hips would have stopped because of such standing in the gap. But we would have been better ministers. Or even priests: literally, those who stand for their people before God. And we would have had more to say to God's people on God's behalf when we gathered for Sunday worship, like Moses come down the mountain, face shining.

Can I sue our younger selves for pastoral malfeasance?

Not for doing nothing—again, prayer was on our list. It just wasn't top of our list. Pastors are paid to pray. Nothing more or less.

Sam Wells writes of the pastoral vocation in a way that Methodists may find odd at first, but we will see to be more congenial with a second look. The pastor, for the Anglican Wells, is a priest. This priestly vocation works in two directions. In one, the priest goes to God on behalf of the people. She bears their complaints. She turns away from the people and toward God saying prayers on their behalf. Methodists sometimes signal this, perhaps unwittingly, by kneeling at the altar during the prayers of the people. In pastoral care we do it by constantly asking what we can pray for on behalf of our people. Without this priestly, prayerful intent we confuse pastoral visitations with social visits. We confuse prayers of the people during church with announcements or community kvetching or sentimentality. That is time in the presence of God. We would do well to take off our shoes.

Annie Dillard, in *Holy the Firm*, speaks of the pastor in her little church in the Pacific Northwest carrying on pastoral prayers like a veritable argument with God, like Jacob wrestling at the Jabbok. If we mean God to act, we will do something similar. One Sunday, praying through the grim litany of cancer, job loss, and grief, the pastor interrupted himself, "Lord, *we pray these same prayers every week!*"[1] Act, God. Now! Amos Wilder once put it unforgettably: prayer is "approaching an open volcano where the world is molten and hearts are sifted. The altar is like a third rail that spatters sparks; the sanctuary is like the chamber next to an atomic oven: there are invisible rays and you leave your watch outside."[2] The pastor, as priest, approaches God in prayer like the burning bush, the chariots of fire, the transfiguration. If it takes a lot to remember that a little bitty church is where this divine theater is playing out, well, it probably took some work too for Moses, Elisha, and Peter.

Such prayer could go wrong. Jaylynn was presiding away once when an interruption came in the form of a raised hand. It wasn't uncommon for someone to stop her wherever she was in the service if they forgot something they meant to say in prayer request time.

"Uh, yes?" Jaylynn said, ever the teacher of elementary school kids she once was.

"We forgot to pray for somethin'."

"OK, what?" Jaylynn was holding the offering plates. The offering having just been collected, they were a bit heavy. Next step was to sing the doxology. It couldn't come soon enough.

"My neighbor's friend's daddy was ridin' on the ridin' mower . . ."

One could tell this was going to end badly.

"And he fell off and cut his arm off and had a heart attack."

The congregation gasped en masse.

"Really?" Jaylynn said. "We'll have to pray for him. Now let's sing the doxology."

Everyone rose, on news of the severed limb-cum-cardiac arrest: "Praise God from whom all blessings flow . . ."

More ordinarily prayers of the people is a time of genuine offering (and in the lady's defense, it was a time of genuine offering for her—played up a little for dramatic effect). We take something tender and true to us and offer it to one another, the minister, and God. And the minister's job is to gather those offerings, like pearls, and set them before the Lord, who already knows our hearts. If

---

1. (New York: Harper & Row, 1988), 88.

2. "Electric Chimes or Rams' Horns" in *Grace Confounding* (Philadelphia: Fortress, 1972), 13.

only we offered things more aimed at soul-level, less predictable than health alerts. The prayers become a litany that reads like the "to-do" list on a hospital wall. Those offerings are precious too, of course, and should never be omitted. We should just add to them: prayers for grace when we're spiritually dry. Prayers for conversion of those we love. Prayers for help when we're overpaid and in spiritual danger. Prayers for help when we're unemployed and in real trouble of another kind. The pastor, of course, is in the best position of all to model this. A priestly position.

Priestly intercession goes another direction as well. We don't just speak to God on behalf of the people, we also speak to the people on behalf of God. This is the scarier one for us (it shouldn't be, but bear with me). We're so rightly afraid of repeating occasions when the church has spoken wrongly, hurtfully on behalf of God that we hesitate to speak of our sermons and liturgy presiding generally as divine speech. But they are! When we preach, God is speaking. Fitfully so—we are sinners standing up and preaching to other sinners. But nonetheless, the church has historically spoken of the Word of God in several forms: fleshed in Jesus, witnessed to in Scripture, proclaimed in church. The pastor in her study, in the sanctuary before worship, in prayer, and in preaching, is speaking words from the Lord. We should watch our tongues. And once in a while when we preach we shouldn't be surprised that it feels like someone *else* is preaching through us—because that's precisely what's happening.

Perhaps the best place to think of this is indeed in pastoral prayer. That is, the *first* place we speak the Lord's words is in prayer. If our attention is directed Godward in prayers of the people, and in all the other prayers, the congregation's attention will also turn Godward, in the prayers, in the rest of the service, and ultimately in the rest of their lives. For prayer is ultimately an inner-Trinitarian conversation into which we creatures are invited. Paul speaks in Romans 8 of the Spirit bearing witness with our spirits that we are children of God (8:15-17). That the groans with which we approach God in prayer are actually the Spirit rumbling within us, speaking to the Father, shaping us into the image of the Son (8:22-23). If we attend to that inner-Trinitarian conversation in pastoral prayer, we'll have a better shot of doing so in preaching and in the rest of our pastoral ministries.

Sarah Coakley, a theologian and Anglican priest at Cambridge University, has written beautifully of the *way* we envision the Trinity. We think of the Father coming "first" somehow, as if in time or rank, the Son "second," and the Spirit "third." In one way this is right—the Father is "first" in order of processions, as long as we are clear there is no "before" the Son—the Father is always begetting the Son and breathing the Spirit. The lockstep ordering is fine as long as it is balanced with other images of the Trinity, for example, that of Romans 8:22-27. Here we think not of who is first, second, third, but *through* the mundane, liturgical practice of prayer. In prayer, especially wordless prayer for Coakley, if we're silent enough, we can hear a conversation *already in progress*. It is as though this conversation is taking place through us. It's the eternal divine discourse between the Father and the Spirit within the triune life. And the Son? That's creation itself, with humanity at its pinnacle, becoming divinized by partaking in this triune communion.

How would this view of the Trinity affect us on Sundays? Well, we'd be more attentive to the divine presence if we had this view in mind. It's like we gather beside a roaring bonfire, or a death drop off a cliff, every Sunday, and mostly don't notice that our life is a few feet from ending. If we thought in Coakley's Trinitarian terms, God wouldn't seem so far off, unaffected, distant. And we'd attend more to the divine presence in our fellow pray-ers—they are creatures in whom the Spirit is also rumbling. At the very least we would approach pastoring as a priestly work, in the best sense: our life is one of going to God on behalf of the people, and then going to the people on behalf of God. Careful now—when you do it, your belly may rumble and your face may shine.

CHAPTER SIX

To the Ends of the Earth

A year or so into her appointment, Jaylynn started getting antsy. "I have *got* to get out of the country," she said.

Evangelicals had taught us both how to do mission trips. She'd been to Bolivia, Costa Rica, Mexico, and Guatemala. I'd been to the latter two plus Honduras. It's a formula really: you announce a trip, send out "support letters," friends and family send checks, and you're off somewhere. You build something, you mingle with the locals, traipse through the tourist sights in garish hiking boots more fabulous than anything your hosts could ever afford. And then come back and show slides about how much good you did. It's simple really.

Do I sound a bit cynical?

The rationale behind such trips is not (or at least it shouldn't be) that they do anything good for the people you go to serve. It's that they do something good for you. Any other argument for them is nonsense. Once in Honduras, a spritely undergraduate proclaimed one evening, "We repaired that lady's water pipe. She has water she didn't have before. That's worth coming down here." Yes, as though she couldn't have had it fixed by a relative in the village. As if our plumbing skills are admirable—we college kids from the United States. As if rural Honduran villagers haven't been making do without do-gooder gringos showing up to feel good about themselves for fixing stuff for them. And worst of all is the breathtaking degree of pride. That student—and all of us really—comes home proudly claiming success for what he's done to the "support" people who paid for him to go. You see the jadedness with these sorts of trips now—in undergraduates who show up at college with long lists of where they've been, already tired of such "experiences." You see it in the field too. A friend went back to Tanzania on his own after being there with a group a few months before. The cement buildings they had so dutifully painted blue had been equally dutifully repainted green by some subsequent group. The hosts have to find something for the "missionaries" to do, or they don't come and bring their spending money for the souvenir stands. On a trip to Uganda once, I noticed a school we visited put out a welcome banner, under which they waved and danced at our arrival. A closer look revealed that the banner was reusable. It didn't mention our group. It just said, "Welcome to our American visitors." An American there longer than our two weeks said the Ugandans call the summer "the American visiting season." It's like a bird migration.

Turns out the Methodists had a long relationship with colleagues in Russia. And a church in the conference was sending a group that summer. Perfect. I'd always been fascinated with the "evil empire," and life behind that iron curtain, even if it was now lifted. Jaylynn just wanted to go and serve anywhere but Zebulon. Living in that cramped rural community ran the risk of clamping down our universe, with the two families in each church and their crops and petty dislikes. Of course we didn't realize we would be bringing our*selves* with us—and we were party to the difficult relationships.

And we did have a marvelous time. Jaylynn and I walked around Red Square on our first wedding anniversary, hoping to find a place to celebrate. We found no eatery at all. Not a lack of any we could afford, but none at all. We had ice cream sandwiches back in the hotel. We saw the Russian Orthodox Cathedral of Christ the Savior, dynamited under Stalin, and rebuilt on state money under Yeltsin and Putin (Russia never has gotten the memo about separation of church and state). We learned about the Orthodox Church—that its onion domes are meant to represent the tongues of fire of Pentecost, and that the magnificent multispired building that served as Tom Brokaw's U.S.S.R. backdrop over the years was indeed a church, not their version of Congress (built to praise the mother of God after a victory over the Kazakhs, of course). I watched for an hour as visitors to Moscow's Tretyakov Gallery stopped in front of Andrei Rublev's icon of the Holy Trinity and crossed themselves. You can try and stamp out Christianity with official atheism, but seventy-five years later, kids will still know what to do in the presence of holiness. Over vodka one night I asked our host, a massive woman named Ina (whom we called Ina the Queena) just how she felt when the U.S.S.R. fell. She had to have been a party member—she'd run something called the Peace Foundation, which hosted us, and had done so since long before 1989. You didn't run anything in the U.S.S.R., let alone something that hosted Westerners, without being a party member. She looked around, and then whispered under her breath, "I felt crushed—I had great hopes for our country." Now *that's* how you lament the fall of an empire. Americans, take notice.

The problem was not the failure of our goals. *Our* lives *were* expanded briefly. So were those of our team members. We took Michael and Betsy, a young married couple, and Elizabeth, a career homemaker and farmer's wife who'd dreamed of going to Russia since studying the language in college and seeing *Doctor*

Zhivago as a teenager. They were thrilled. The community jumped in to support us. They prayed in our absence and heard stories upon our return. They were nothing if not supportive.

But they did ask questions.

"Why are we serving people halfway around the world when we got needy people here in Zebulon?"

It was a good question, which we vanquished with typical aplomb. "We learn to serve there so we come back here with new eyes to see need," I said. They blinked at me. Not buying it.

"This models reconciliation with our former enemies," Jaylynn said. More blinking. Like there aren't enough historic enemies in rural North Carolina to take several lifetimes to patch up. Some of the Johnstons and the Vogels hadn't spoken in years. And we're not even onto black and white people yet.

I think they just plugged in their own expectations of "mission trip." On the train between Moscow and our destination, Michael leaned over to us one night to say something risky.

"They won't believe us back home," he said.

Why?

"Cause this don't seem like no missionary trip." He was right. Back in Zebulon one of the basic tenets of Christianity was that one didn't drink (up there with not cussing. Smoking, not surprisingly given the local economy, was OK.). Michael and others usually drank out of sight of their pastor. Now, in Russia, on a mission trip, he was drinking with his pastor (or at least with her husband), when back home he was barely legally of age. Every night we were wined and dined and entertained by singing or dancing. This was a trip designed in the 1970s to receive American visitors, and then send them back determined not to let their government bomb the bejesus out of the little Soviet orphans they'd met. We heard story after story of people who had come to realize they were friends and so roared back home and advocated for nuclear disarmament. It didn't take much of this to be suspicious. But mainline churches are not often known for such geopolitical savvy.

When I got home I phoned a relative of mine who has made a living studying Russian language, politics, and culture. He's spent his life translating documents from Russian in order to help Western academics learn what their enemies are up to. These skills are a bit less useful when Google can do the same thing for you, but never mind. It's always been cool to think the CIA must have a file on him.

"So what does a Russian organization called 'The Peace Foundation' suggest to you?"

"A commie front." This man is not a conservative.

"Really? They seemed very nice."

"Yeah, they would. They wanted something from you. What were they like when you visited?"

I remembered the parties and tours and glad handing. The goal of this U.S.S.R.-era fossil had changed little: it was to have us call our representatives when we got back. And our church's relationship with it showed very little awareness of their intentions. Sure you can meet with enemies. But you can't let yourself be used unawares.

My greatest fear about the mission trip was that it hurt Michael and Betsy's marriage. He partook of the alcohol along with us. It's Russia, they drink vodka like water (in fact the word *vodka* means "little water" in Russian). We'd not have done this back home, being good Methodists. But it felt right to drink in Russia somehow, just accepting their hospitality. I first learned on a trip to Guatemala (evangelical globe-trotters that we were) that you eat and drink what's set before you. In some places this was bugs. In Russia it was "little water."

Betsy abstained. Asked upon our return what should have been different about the trip, the young bride pursed her lips, "There was a little too much drinkin' going on." She must have known more about Michael's history than she was letting on. In Russia we hadn't caroused, we'd just drunk a little at dinner with our hosts, and this had been enough for her to worry.

As well she should have. Michael took back to ways he'd once left behind when he'd joined the church—drinking and partying. Their fragile marriage started to fray, then simply shattered. Betsy never blamed us for this. But maybe she didn't have to.

St. Augustine has an enormously sanguine view of leadership. Leaders, for his reading of the Bible, have to be the best repenters around. For the human exemplars we have in Scripture are people like David and Paul. They are outrageous, unbelievable sinners. David, the warrior prince, womanizer, murderer. Paul the murdering archenemy of the early church. Both leave us models for repentance and conversion in places like Psalm 51 and Acts 9. And those conversions, that *metanoia*, that turning around, would never have been so impressive had they not been such remarkable sinners.

This is a point of hope for Christian ministers. With the Russia trip we launched an endeavor that we meant for the good of our own souls and that of our churches. They went along because they're loyal church people. And it turns out not for good, and maybe even for harm.

If there's one area in which pastors should lead the congregation, we should lead in repenting. Especially in repenting of shrugging off hard questions and criticisms from the very people we serve. In this case at least, the pointed questions from laypeople were exactly on target. We did have needy people in Zebulon, and it would have been a better use of resources all around to serve without getting on two overnight international flights. This is my great fear— that pastoral ministry as such becomes something done for the minister, and not for the church. That may be us mainline ministers at our worst.

And yet. Does not our God bring springs from dry desert? We met some orphans on that trip. These were the very people we actually went to serve. We volunteered at an orphanage in the little town of Orel, three hours southwest of Moscow. The town was so remote that when Methodists first started coming, the locals said the last foreigners they'd seen there were Nazis. Ina the Queena told us of the pride that made her heart burst when a Soviet soldier scaled the last standing building in town to wave the hammer and sickle in victory after the Germans were finally repulsed. You won't be surprised to learn that the hammer and sickle symbol on lampposts and the statue of Lenin never quite got taken down in Orel.

These orphans had been abandoned, God knows how long ago. Their parents left them in shame, and no one would adopt them, largely for some odd taboo in Russian culture against adoption. Their best hope was to be drafted into the military, to avoid being beaten to death in one of that army's harsh hazing rituals, and hopefully able after to make a life for themselves. Their service would likely be in Chechnya (where, one tour guide told us, the people had always been a problem. "They have hot blood," she said. Maybe that was just the best the translator could do.). One boy had a heart condition, and knew he couldn't even qualify for the army—his future was bleak indeed. It would not be an easy road for any of them. They seemed to know it. The eight-year-olds smoked two packs a day. Even our North Carolinian parishioners gasped when they heard that.

I spent the week wrestling with them. They climbed all over me. I'd spin them around on my shoulders, turn them upside down, let them jump on me and clobber me. In those moments I felt like I'd never seen happier kids. A big ole Methodist preacher from North Carolina with an expanding waistline could, apparently, do something useful on the mission field after all.

One of the Russian caregivers interpreted the whole thing to me later. These were boys with no father, no memory of a father, no masculine touch that was peaceful. I became that, at least for a little while.

Was it worth it? A church's whole resources to fly five of its members overseas for two weeks of wrestling with fatherless boys?

Maybe. Who can count as the Lord counts?

Just before we left we found out we were pregnant. With the first of three boys. With whom I hope to spend the rest of my life wrestling.

CHAPTER SEVEN

Blessed Be the Lord, Who Trains My Hands for War

W ant to see my AK-47?" No, we weren't still in Russia, home of the Kalashnikov, we were back in rural North Carolina.

What?! I thought. "Are those things even legal, Bob?" He had multiple and seemingly contradictory answers ready. "Oh, yeah. It's only got a ten-bullet clip. It's made in China. Plus I got it at a gun show."

The first rationale of the three offered for the legality of this particular arsenal was once the only one that mattered. But that was before the expiration of the automatic weapon ban in 2004. Today someone could much more easily purchase the civilian version of a military-style assault rifle with far more than ten bullets and have that ready to show their presumably liberal, antigun preacher's husband when he comes over. At this writing in 2009, there have been three murderous shooting sprees in the news in the last four days.

It was an impressive device, I had to admit. When I praised it he begged off: "You've got to see what Bill's got."

This conversation about gun ownership doesn't take place in a vacuum. People who live in more urbane places than Zebulon assume that those who own armories are knuckle-dragging Neanderthals. These guys were among the best-educated and most wealthy parishioners in our churches. And—note this—among the least temperamental. These are not violent people. They are hunters and gun-lovers, not people who shoot at other people. I wouldn't have known the difference had I not spent time with them.

This is not to say that there is not violence just beneath the surface in many such rural communities. It's not too long ago or too far away that being the wrong race and saying the wrong thing could get you lynched in such a place.[1] Jeremy Troxler, the director of the thriving rural churches initiative at Duke Divinity School, puts it this way, speaking of the New Testament's original accursed place: Nazareth. "Nothing good can come out of Nazareth," it was said—until Jesus did. Troxler writes, "Those of us who've grown up in Nazareth know that it has its challenges. We've seen some of the violence that simmers beneath the surface of civility, the willingness to draw hard lines between insider and outsider, the family identities that can crush true expression of self, the thinly veiled prejudice propped up with a Proverb. Jesus had to rescue some of us from that."[2] My friends, Jaylynn's parishioners in Zebulon, were all military men. There was a time, I imagine, when any one of them could've handled himself in a bar fight, just as they once *did* handle themselves with Vietcong.

I couldn't resist. I went over to Bill's place. And sure enough, he had enough weapons to defend the Alamo. And those were only the ones visible. He laughed when I teased him about their number. "You ain't seen nothing. Go see what Mike's got."

I never got to Mike's place. I'm told the guns filled an entire floor. Not just a gun case or a cabinet, but an entire level of house. He was sitting on a real armory, of the sort that could stock a militia. No wonder Democrats rarely stand a chance out here. On a trip back during the 2008 election campaign, we counted as many Confederate flags as Obama signs.

But here's what's scarier than that: the arrogance with which such people are derided from places like Durham and Chicago. These men were among the gentlest I've ever known. But here's the ambiguity: they're the most inclined to believe it when Fox News says Obama wants to take their guns away. Weird.

Having lived and preached among avid gun-owners while a pastor in rural North Carolina, I am more sympathetic with their arguments than I once was. These guys know how to handle guns. They're stored properly, locked in a safe where thieves (or even their owner) couldn't get them if his house were robbed. These guys are all ex-military and know from experience how dangerous such weapons are, and how important it is to use them properly. They all hunt. Some of them don't hunt for more deer than they'll eat in a given winter. The world will not be less safe if Bob can have more firepower—strange as it is to hear myself say that. Chad Mason, a hunter and Mennonite pastor, has written that many gun owners "do not see a weapon when we look at a gun. Rather, we see a

---

1. This is no idle claim. See Tim Tyson's justly celebrated *Blood Done Sign My Name* (New York: Three Rivers Press, 2005).

2. Jeremy Troxler's sermon "Nazareth" is available at http://www.divinity.duke.edu /programs/trc/writings/document_view.

piece of recreational equipment not much different from a pair of skis or a motor-cycle, except that a gun seems, to us, less dangerous."[3] Sure enough—America's rate of gun deaths per year sounds outrageously high, until you compare it with the number of deaths from, say, traffic accidents.

One time at the Branch Ranch a rabid raccoon attacked one of our dogs. I asked another church member if I should buy a rifle of some sort. He looked me up and down and regarded me bemusedly. "Naw, you'd just hurt yourself or some-one else. If you have another attack raccoon, just call me." I would have. Perhaps the community was even safer than it would have been without Bob's gun own-ership. Of course with an AK-47 with ten bullets or now with one with thirty, Bob could mow down a brigade of attack raccoons marching in Napoleonic mil-itary formation.

Which is one less thing to worry about.

It's in university-educated people's blood to make fun of people who bear arms. And it's in theirs to take offense at us. But what else are they supposed to do for entertainment? Drive to the museum in Raleigh? Sit around watching local sports, getting fatter? Hauerwas tells the story in his forthcoming memoir about his father, a bricklayer, who made him a beautiful rifle for a gift.[4] Stan, then a Yale student, tried to admire it, before saying, "You know we're going to have to take these things away from you people." What a little snot, he now sees, to take a precious handmade gift, an expression of his father's very self, and spit all over it. Later he asked for the rifle from his father and gave it to a hunting friend. Gun owning is integral to all sorts of other practices in places like Zebulon. It's what fathers teach sons. It's what military men learn professionally. Police too. It's weekend entertainment—of the sort that allows men to traipse off in the woods together and communicate in ways they can't just sitting around. It scares liberals like me from places like Durham. And it shouldn't.

Once a man named Curran from one of our churches asked me to come see something. He'd killed an eight-point buck, a marvelous creature, which hung upside down from his barn. He showed me how to count the points. Showed me how he'd gutted him and was letting the blood drain out. Its eyes were open. It looked alive.

"Some people shoot these things from the road, cut off their horns, and leave 'em there to rot," he said, with disgust. "Usually I don't shoot at all. I just like to go out in the woods and look at 'em." This time he'd shot. The beast, now dead, now an occasion of conversation and the passing on of wisdom, even if of a strange sort, was beautiful. And there are presently too many of them in our woods in this part of the country. They jump out in front of cars and kill people.

Once another parishioner, a leading citizen and elected official, asked if I liked to shoot, and if so would I come over and shoot skeet with him sometime.

---

3. "Armed and Defenseless," *Christian Century* 123, no. 13 (June 27, 2006): 9.

4. Stanley Hauerwas, *Hannah's Child* (Grand Rapids: Eerdmans, 2010).

I hadn't processed through all the above yet, so I paused, and then said, "Well, maybe, I'm not so sure." He let it go, and never offered again. All he meant was he'd fire clay disks in the air and we'd blast 'em. It'd have been an occasion to talk, get to know each other, even learn about what our lives outside of church were like. He noticed my hesitation, even discomfort, and let it go. I never had that opportunity back.

Wouldn't the incarnation—God's enfleshment among us in Christ—suggest I ought to have gone? God's willingness to be with us in a strange medium ought to send God's people scurrying to be with others in places that are equally strange to us. Normally for kids from suburban privilege that means a need to go into places of poverty, even destitution. But for me, one time, it meant shooting skeet with a good ole boy politician. And I blew it.

CHAPTER EIGHT

Being Buried with Saints

The entertainment in Zebulon was not all prehistoric. One family that became particularly close to us had us over for their Super Bowl party. It was the infamous year when Janet Jackson had what we would all come to call her "wardrobe malfunction," baring her breast for hundreds of millions of viewers to see. Right before that happened, Jaylynn and I announced to the youth group there gathered, "Janet's still cool." She was, for a few minutes more. Maybe we'd been thinking of the previous year's Super Bowl party when the youth asked us, "Who are *these* guys?" as U2 bounded onto the stage. Ouch.

Another church member among the hosts that night was on his first date since his wife died. We all spent the night trying to gauge how they took to one another. Well enough, but without deep chemistry. We'd keep praying.

While I was immersed in such deep and pious thoughts, one of the hosts' children came up to me and said, "Pastor Jason, how many beers have you had?" effectively cutting me off faster than any glance from my wife could have. "Go ask your dad how many he's had," I said. Actually I didn't.

It strikes me how ordinary this interaction was. Fun, useless, good for nothing, as all parties must be. As worship must be too, actually.[1]

Worship is productive of nothing. We don't go out having accomplished something, built something, made something, even of ourselves. Most Sundays we don't come out holier or more learned than we came in. That hour did nothing, precisely zero, good for the world. Except allow for worship. And let us realign our lives with the grain of the cosmos. Remind us that we're poor sinners,

---

1. See Marva Dawn, *A Royal "Waste" of Time: The Splendor of Worshiping God and Being Church for the World* (Grand Rapids: Eerdmans, 1999).

creatures in need of grace. And that God met this need before we could even express it with his death and resurrection. Bill Gates is right when he says church is a poor use of time.[2] It's very inefficient. In the best sense.

This kind of uselessness is hard for type-A achievers. Hard-driven people want time to be productive. Even parties among our graduate school friends usually involved the same conversations over academic things conducted in another measure—with alcohol as lubricant (it's been described as "moasting"—boasting about who has the most to complain about. It's a contact sport.). Here, talking to the six-year-olds about my alcohol intake, having the same conversations with church people we normally have on Sundays except trying to think of something to say about Kid Rock (before even Janet came on), was awkward. Aren't parties always? But more so with parishioners. And it was glorious, in a useless sort of way.

A previous gathering for worship was for that same widower on the death of his wife, Carrie, some years before. She did everything at the church: played piano, directed the choir (such as it was), helped with the youth, cooked casseroles, counseled Jaylynn when as a new pastor she didn't know which way was up. It was hard to imagine the church without her. But we had known she was deteriorating. She'd beaten cancer before but then it beat her, coming back with a vengeance. The last I saw her I shouldn't have: her hair was gone, her body shriveled already, as though dieting to fit into a smaller coffin. But when I asked how she was, she said, "Oh, purty good," like she always did. I should have let myself remember her beautiful, like the obituary photos do.

Jaylynn's preaching of Carrie's funeral was one of the highlights of our time in Zebulon, or in all of ministry really. Carrie had invited a black minister friend to read Scripture—surely one of the only times a black man had been at that church, let alone stood in its pulpit. This at a church where the pianist, generations before, used to knit robes for the Klan—it was Carrie who once told us. Generations later she sat on that piano bench Sunday after Sunday, and now during her own funeral she was inviting black people in, and her heart would have roared with pride to have them stay and bring their kids. "Just like her to be thinking about her church's faithfulness even after her death," Jaylynn said.

My wife preached her heart out, largely using Carrie's own preaching directives—what verses to cite, bits of Wesley to quote, what hymns to sing. And afterward as she processed out, the widower wept openly, sobbing, gasping for air. Jaylynn held his hand so tightly they could have made a diamond together. I stood outside in the rain rocking our firstborn in his removable car seat. To live in a community like this! Where people know one another well enough to mourn this well! There were as many people outside the little white church that day as in, in the rain no less, worshiping outside like the church did at its inception, when the people began to meet to marry and bury and baptize and break

---

2. *Time* 149, no. 2 (January 13, 1997).

bread and worship. They laid Carrie to rest, Jaylynn went home to collapse with exhaustion and grief, and we showed up again the next Sunday.

And that is why the small church is God's primary way of saving the world. Carrie could have been a member at big old Community Baptist in Danville, a leader there even. She'd have been entertained more there, sure enough, so would her kids. But who would have done her funeral? Held her husband's hand as he sobbed? Comforted her kids and mother in the coming days? Remembered to go to her grave when they're back in town? Who?

The small church is the best-kept secret in mainline Protestantism.[3] We have loads of such churches. They have their faults, Lord knows, their psychoses even. Evangelism happens in greater numbers at big churches, no doubt. More people are served through large church's dynamic ministries. Nobody's going to film small-church worship and put it on cable or the Internet, or expand it to multisite worship settings.

But Carrie knew where she was going to be buried. So did everyone else at that church. She knew who would weep at her funeral and what stories they'd tell. She could see the end of her life long before she knew when it was coming. And when it came too soon, she knew her widower and children would be cared for. They wouldn't be the only ones who'd have to remember stories about Carrie. Dozens of others would help.

I have no idea where I'll be buried. I'm a creature of large urban and university churches. These don't have cemeteries. But Carrie's husband, the heartbroken widower, can go back in full confidence that he and his children will be buried beside her, in the church's cemetery, beside that white clapboard (OK, it's vinyl siding really) church where they praised Jesus every Sunday. They'll have some cranks and some nuts buried near them. People they probably avoided at the potlucks. Also present and ready for duty are friends whom they're already eager to spend eternity with even before everybody's sanctified. They're all there. And that's beautiful.

Once I became a pastor of my own flock I would often stroll in my own church's cemetery. I've found myself doing this in strange cemeteries when I'm traveling. If I'm in an unfamiliar town and have time to kill, the graveyard is a great place to do it. You learn so much. It's not at all uncommon to find a headstone for a father, with a mother beside, and then five, six, seven or more little stones with infant children. Children died at birth and in infancy so often. There's little sign of the grief, less of the smarmy slogans we often send the dead to rest underneath. Just a quiet witness to agony in a time before child mortality became uncommon. Sometimes such stones will simply say "With Jesus." Older,

---

3. In a terrific editorial, the author talks about stumbling back to church as she looked for someone to be nice to her for less than the therapist's $125 an hour. She found it in the passing of the peace. We get a lot right: V. C. Chickering, "Church Junkie," *Washington Post* (April 26, 2009).

Puritan stones, carved in slate in New England graveyards have images of skulls, meant to terrify rather than comfort. "What you are, I was once; what I am, you will be," one's Latin inscription reads.

At Beech Grove I would look at the family names, identical to those I pastored now, and wonder about the connections: parents? Uncles? Cousins? There was no doubt they were kin. The stones would ask, "Are you being faithful to my children?" Some of those children seemed perennially annoyed with me (and vice versa). The silent witness of the stones reminded me that they and their families had been contributors to that community for a long time. Their ancestors were out back, forever "at church" in a way, testifying to their hope of Jesus' return and their bodily resurrection with a burial in a churchyard. Somehow those walks made me more ready to be pastorally attentive to their descendants who were walking around above ground. It sent me back to my study with more energy to prepare to preach and teach.

There was a sense in which I was pastor to these souls too, though they now rest. G. K. Chesterton talks about tradition as the "democracy of the dead." Even those below ground get a vote on what Christians ought to think. There are, indeed, more of them than there are of us, so they usually override us among the living. That's real democracy, unlike negligence of the dead by "the arrogant oligarchy that happens to be walking about above ground."

Here's the thing—what about when the dead *were* wrong?

A pastor friend of mine had a church in West Tennessee once. He called me up one day, practically hollering, "There are Byassees in my churchyard." So we went to see him, and sure enough, there was my last name. We don't know how the people were related to me, but clearly they were. Only one Huguenot with that name came to America—John Byassee, to Virginia, in 1690. My great-great-great-grandfather had nineteen kids. They scattered, and we don't know our distant cousins, including, perhaps, this man, who lived and died in the same town as my grandfather. In an odd way, my pastor friend's care of his people there was like his care for me as his friend.

Later he moved back to North Carolina, as I did. He does the rural pastorate thing right—raises his own chickens and grows squash. His church grows by a little, not a lot. And he competently and lovingly serves them well.

One day for a funeral a fellow seminary classmate of ours showed up at his church for a funeral. "She was my aunt," he explained. "I got relatives all over this churchyard." Sure enough he did. So do all of us.

The graveyard at this particular little church is covered over with sand, like a bit of the beach was dislodged by plate tectonics and dropped off in the Piedmont of North Carolina. Gleaming white is a startling sight in former tobacco country.

Beech Grove had once threatened to fill their cemetery with sand. The United Methodist Men proposed it, but the United Methodist Women got word of it and put the kibosh on it.

"Don't have to mow that way," one pro-sand man explained then. His wife was in the United Methodist Women. She won.

"Sure is hell on the gravediggers," my friend told us when we asked about the sand in his church's graveyard.

I watched as our kids played in the sand like they were at the beach. Surely if the dead knew, they wouldn't mind. Few Southerners come from anywhere other than these small, rural churches.

There's precisely the rub. My ancestors in West Tennessee, his in central North Carolina, were not above reproach. They no doubt fought for the Confederacy. Little flags (not the rebel flag—these organizations have figured out how to avoid public controversy) wave over some of those graves, tended by various associations for remembering Dixie's dead. Buried slaves don't get such care. They rarely got stones. But you can bet they're there, as they were with the Southern whites in life.

Who brings this up when we talk of the democracy of the dead?

That's why it matters so much to be buried in a church yard. The bodies of the saints are now quite literally under the shadow of the cross. If there is any mercy for them it is a mercy outside of us, not owed to us, one that is altogether grace and undeserved. And need I even make this connection? If there is any mercy for *us*, it is likely for sins so close we cannot see them either, and it is outside of us, not owed to us, altogether grace and undeserved. Later generations will cluck their tongues at us too—for who knows what? "How could they not have known better?" And we will have no defense. Except Jesus.

The novelist Wendell Berry's main character in *Jayber Crow* is both a barber and an undertaker. He likes to spend time in graveyards reflecting on precisely these things. He *belongs* to those underground in the deepest sense, and they to him, with all the dread and glory that such membership entails. "This grief had something in it of generosity, some nearness to joy. In a strange way it added to me what I had lost. . . . The world as it is would always be a reminder of the world that was, and of the world that is to come."[4]

Jaylynn and I have no idea where we'll be buried. Or, as it is with big churches, even whether we will be buried. They might just turn us into ash and stuff us in a bowl in a wall by a bench or spread us at a garden or the beach, where we'll go as unvisited as most church graveyards. Is it possible to belong anyplace without knowing you'll be, quite literally, planted there? Who has mercy on you without a plot to walk over you, or sand for kids to play in over your coffin?

---

4. Wendall Berry, *Jayber Crow* (Berkeley: Counterpoint, 2000), 132.

CHAPTER NINE

Take Thou Authority

I took my own first church appointment because I needed the money. Why didn't anyone tell me finances would be so tight out of seminary? OK, they told me we'd make no money, but I didn't realize that'd mean so *little* "no money." As a student I had a salary of zero, and did OK (they also didn't tell me you have to pay those loans back. Or they did, but I wasn't listening.). Then my minister-wife was to receive a salary of some $30,000, which sounded like a lot more than zero. "We might buy a boat or a beach house," I told her confidently— ridiculously, as it turned out. A year in and we had more debts than we'd started with. I wasn't going to be a stay-at-home graduate school student and husband for long (plus I couldn't even do the laundry).

Seminary indebtedness is becoming an increasing problem for young ministers. Most of their churches don't know about it. Our culture keeps a hush on any talk about money—we'd sooner tell our sexual exploits in public than reveal the contents of our bank accounts. But student loan repayments are a real problem. The $400 per month we have to pay for the next twenty years means we're starting in a salary hole—whatever we look to bring in, after taxes, that amount comes off the top. And the salary already isn't high. And how exactly are we supposed to pay for our own kids' education?

Such loan repayments are similar to the way Spaniards treat their bulls before bullfighters go in to fight them. That bull already has several spikes sticking out of its neck and a spear thrust in between its shoulder blades. Before the bullfighter ever enters, the bull is already slowly dying of blood loss. Without that advantage we'd have a lot more dead bullfighters.

Two checks a month to the student loan people left us feeling like we were slowly bleeding to death. And our parishes never knew it.

We'd been at Buelah and Rehobeth for a year. I'd started out going to every service. Then we both noticed hearing the same sermon the second time around when you'd already edited it and pitched in a few of its key ideas was a bit tedious (even with Jaylynn preaching). So I went to one church a Sunday, alternating between the two (another advantage of pastoral husbandship—no one questions these decisions). Sundays got progressively more depressing. It was the same people every week. Forever. I could do something here. But what? Plus we were just barely getting by.

Money's not the only reason I sought that calling, though. Graduate school can be soul destroying. This is ironic—I was studying theology, the study of the way God meets and blows life into souls, not how he ruins them. But there I was reading hundreds of pages a week, reading like a bulimic eats, getting ready for PhD seminars. These would come and go in three hours, I'd be sure to make a comment smart enough to indicate to the professor I'd read and digested what was said before I hurled it, and another week would be over. "I'm depressed," I told Jaylynn one night. "What am I doing that has any lasting impact on the world? I mean, if I died, who would come to the funeral?"

"My parishioners at Buelah?" she ventured. Not helpful. She was admitting that everyone at the grad school would be busy studying that day.

"What if I took a church?" I asked, almost despite myself. For some graduate students, pastors of churches are lesser creatures. Those who could, did PhD work. The parish was the minor leagues, academic work the big leagues. "Publish or parish," theological academics joke, in a play on secular academia's "publish or perish." Pastoring is an admission of unclear thinking, or excessive sappiness, or loving Jesus: all mistakes. Plus it took time. Lots of time. "Never let a professor know you didn't do something because of your church," one professor-confidant suggested. "Never." I almost did once. "Missed you at the lecture yesterday," a professor said, referring to a visitor to Durham all the way from Birmingham, England, an expert in patristics, which I was studying. My absence had been noticed. I almost said, "Yeah, I was at a hearing for a troubled teenager at my church because the county is thinking about ruling that his grandmother is ill equipped to care for him and wants to make him a ward of the state." I'll leave to you to decide which was the more important activity. But I didn't say that. I'd been warned.

The distinction in worlds between Zebulon County and Duke was that of perfect opposition. Out there at Zebulon I could talk as Southern as I could and still sound like a Yankee to everybody else. Could be as practical as you please and not apologize for it. Could sit and stare at a sunset just because it was there. Could listen for hours to a tobacco farmer talk about Brightleaf and curing in barns and the odd carcinogens they had to take out while leaving others in. And it was all good. At Duke I could argue about whether Social Trinitarianism was a good idea or whether Barth had appropriated Hegel properly, and it made sense to do that. Neither place spoke the other's language. But one was supposed to provide preachers to the other, and the other was supposed to provide preachers-in-training to the one. How exactly does that work again?

Jaylynn said, "That's a great idea!" She responded to my question about whether I should be a pastor with more warmth than anything I'd told her about Augustine over the past year. "The current pastor is leaving Beech Grove. It's part time. It could be perfect. Let me ask around to find out more." That was all she needed to say.

It was one of the best conversations I ever had. Unplanned, based on a spasm of an idea born of my feeling squeezed and depressed in a PhD program and academic career that seemed to be going nowhere fast. Pure serendipity. Grace. That church would become a people I love like my mother, like my child, joined to me and I to them because of an offhand comment while my wife and I were getting into our pajamas one night.

In my denomination's ordination service, immediately after the ancient rite of the laying on of hands, the bishop presents the newly ordained with a Bible and intones these sacred words: "Take thou authority." It's an appropriate charge. To pastor a church is an enormous amount of authority: to grant life or to take it (please God let us grant life). But it's not one's personal authority—the bishop is just a bishop of the church catholic, not the founder of a personal religion. The ordinand is one of a legion of Methodist preachers, in line with previous preachers all the way back to Jesus. Her or his individuality (memoirs aside) is not what's emphasized here. It is the authority of this book, bearing witness to this Savior, in this church.

None of us could wear this mantle without the Spirit's steel in our spines.

CHAPTER TEN

God, Who Gives Life to the Dead and Calls into Existence Things That Do Not Exist[1]

My first trip to Beech Grove was as a visiting preacher. I lazy-day'd down winding Beech Grove Road with no idea how many times I would burn down that road at hazardous speed over the next two years, lest my church start worship without me and learn just how dispensable I was. The grove is, indeed, surrounded by trees, but not actually beeches, more pines. Methodists like naming things for geography. Incorrect geography. My wife grew up at Sierra Vista UMC in San Angelo, Texas. "Sierra Vista" means "Mountain view" in Spanish. There are no mountains in this part of West Texas. In a land as flat as thin paper, there is a view, I guess, just not of much one would want to look at. Maybe we like naming ourselves after *somebody's* geography. Just not ours.

Driving in for that first guest gig, I noticed the goats across the street, the veranda-fronted mansions, the crumbling adobelike structures, the grinding gap between rich and poor in one of North Carolina's poorest counties. And I noticed the humble, unassuming, but confident red brick, white-columned Beech Grove UMC. Its people were friendly, not smarmy, but inviting. The music

---

1. Romans 4:17.

was spiritually serious, good even, as its dedicated musicians pounded out Jesus hymns on the piano. One of the blue-clad choristers whom I would come to call "the blue people" was named Alan Jackson. "Really? You must like country music," I said, wincing, sure he'd heard this joke twice that morning already.

"What do you mean?" His blank face told me that Alan is a straitlaced guy, and apparently no fan of country music. He never did like my jokes.

The church was great that Sunday. They (except for Alan) laughed at the jokes and nodded at the profound stuff. I'd had a great time, dressing up like an important person, preparing all week to say words that mattered, doing so with aplomb.

But the then-pastor stiffed me on the payment—promised me fifty bucks, which never came. Dang. Twenty hours of preaching preparation (or ten. OK, four) wasted.[2]

Now I'd be back as pastor. I guess I was going to get them to pay me one way or the other. It was my first meeting with the committee that greeted me, and Kate was among the people there. "I want to rest under the weight of this," I said, as Kate smiled and nodded. The others mostly eyed me warily, but Kate was supportive right away. She would remain one of my biggest sources of constancy. We had no idea her daughter would almost die in a car wreck a few years later, after I left the church. Life has that odd way of being lived forward and only being intelligible backward.

One Sunday I was preaching away when I noticed one of the older couples in front of me in some distress. Elizabeth was trying to wake her husband, whose dozing during my sermons was not uncommon, but whose inability to wake up was.

"I'm going to call a time-out," I said. "Elizabeth, do you need some help?"

"I think I do."

The church leapt into action. Some of it was haphazard—like all of my actions. Where should I stand? Up here at the pulpit? Down there near the people? Do I take my robe off? Why was I thinking about this so much? No one else was noticing how worthless I was. What difference did it make *where* I was worthless?

Kate was anything but worthless. Her training as a nurse was perfect. Someone went to get her in the nursery, where she spent far more time caring for others' kids than anyone had ever done for her. She wasn't keeping score.

"Jonathan!" She hollered, all but ordering him to wake up. "He's got a pulse. Jonathan!" Now to me: "Call 9-1-1!" Ah ha! Something I could do.

---

2. My closest friend as a parishioner, Mamie, tells the story differently. She claims I said, "The chance to preach is all the payment I need." I'm sure I said something meant to indicate the money wasn't the most important thing to me, but to remember me saying something that pious is grading on the curve. "You had my heart then," she says. Do you see what grace they dole out in such places?

Jonathan was fine. He faints sometimes. He did that day in church. He's over ninety now, one of the oldest men in the church. He and Elizabeth married when he was a teacher and she a high school student. These days that sort of thing would get you locked up. Back then it made them the county's it-couple of the year. It didn't hurt that Elizabeth was a looker. Still is. I told her so once, that she was a beautiful older woman (can't remember why I thought this was a good idea). Next time she saw me was in the grocery store. "Hi, handsome," she said. I blushed. Loud.

Kate was in charge of the church that day, more than any preacher or other attender. She's in charge of her house, her professional life. But her daughter was outside her grasp that night on the narrow roads of the county highways. Her daughter was lucky to live, and even to recover fully. "You probably think it's funny that I have purple hair," she told me when I went back once. Funny what she thought I would be thinking about. I was just glad I hadn't been asked back to do her daughter's funeral.

The night of that first meeting with the committee, all these unknowns of fragility and grace were yet to come. I had no idea that Kate would burn herself so deeply into my memory when she nodded and smiled politely at that introductory meeting. And we got to know each other probably less than I got to know anyone else in the room.

On the way out of church after the emergency, Bob shook my hand, did the obligatory thanks for the sermon, heard me admit to being a bit distracted delivering it (the sounds of EMTs and their CBs in the next room will do that to you). "You're a good leader," he said, delivering the undeserved compliment I least expected. I've already said how useless I felt—be-robed up there at the pulpit, unable to revive anybody. All I did was notice Jonathan was asleep and Elizabeth was having a harder time waking him than usual. I called a halt to worship and people went running to find Kate. I felt like a second appendix.

But maybe that's what leadership is, in the church or outside. Noticing. Calling a halt when necessary. And then getting out of the way of people who know what they're doing. I'll take Bob's word for it.

And I am glad we kept going with worship, even with Jonathan being worked on next door. When I go down someday, I hope it'll be in church. I hope they'll keep singing. How much sweeter a sound is that than the beeps and crackles of machines. It's reason enough to want to increase the number of hours one spends in church per week, just to up the likelihood a little.

CHAPTER ELEVEN

Oh Yes, You Did Laugh[1]

It's been five years since I left Beech Grove. I visited recently and soaked up their warmth like a sunflower liberated from the shade. They hugged me, told me they missed and loved me, remembered stories from our time together. It was a moment of eschatological anticipation (as we say at the divinity school) or a little like heaven, as they say in Zebulon. I shouldn't have been surprised to see how much everyone has aged. There've been major surgeries, and one man is in serious trouble with cancer. One widow moved away to live with her daughters—eye trouble, can't drive herself anymore. Two are more frail, forgetful, trembling, nervous now, but still coming on Sundays. Several have gone on to be with the Lord. We're all exactly five years closer.

But some of the oldest folks have signs of new life. My friend Michael has a "special friend," in the language of dating elderly people. He has bandages covering more skin cancer even than he had when I was there. His hands shake more. He forgets words in mid-sentence. He still has his Hemingwaylike beard, and, his girlfriend told me, his "garden," which seems to me indistinguishable from a full-grown farm ("Want some corn?" he'd ask, before throwing a bucketful into my car). But he has a special friend now. Someone to share the lazy afternoons and the Sunday pew with.

Another parishioner and older woman, named Edith, also has such a friend. She didn't tell me herself. Someone told on her. "Ms. Edith sits in a different pew!" he reported, before waiting for my reaction to this earthquake. "Wow. How could that happen?" "Well, she has a special friend, and he likes sitting in the back." It must be love.

---

1. Genesis 18:15.

Another old man at Beech Grove told me that he missed sex after his wife died. "You know they got that Viagra now," he said, leaving me feeling decidedly awkward. I'd figured old people gave up sex like middle-aged men must eventually give up basketball—without too much reflection, but with the realization the body just can't take it or doesn't enjoy it anymore.

Those of us who advocate for more frequent celebration of communion (as Luther, Calvin, and Wesley all did) sometimes use an analogy. When a parishioner argues, "It won't be as special if it's done too often," the ready answer is, "Well, is intimacy with a beloved worse because done too often?" Perhaps this works better with hormone-charged youth groups or college fellowships. Because when Jaylynn and I broke the argument open with middle-aged ladies at one of our churches, they all paused. "Sex once a quarter, as often as we have communion? That sounds about right."

Then the really pressing question—why the hell do I care about the sex lives of my older parishioners? It may be because church is sexy (I'm almost tempted to reverse it—sex is churchy). Sarah Coakley, whom I've mentioned before, likes to reverse Freud. If he thought talk about God was really repressed talk about sex, he was almost exactly wrong: talk about sex is actually repressed talk about God. Church is erotic, in a chaste sort of way. Protestants' great gift to the church universal—the hymn—is surprisingly erotically charged when done right. In summer revivals in small Southern churches, the piano belting a tune and all singing like David before the Lord, people get saved not just because of manipulation but because the experience is physically glorious—no wonder the stories are legion of kids spooning in the woods, or of famous entertainers getting their start in little backwoods hymnsings. It happens.

I bumped into this sex-God connection in weird ways. At a funeral home visitation, chatting up the second wife of a son of the deceased (each wife got younger. Why is my gender so predictable?) I realized she was flirting with me. This was a new experience. I didn't get this with the old ladies at the church, with whom things were more obviously chaste. Another time a troubled young woman in financial need came to the church, likely to ask help feeding one of her many kids, each by different husbands. I realized as she played the emotional victim in my office there was an erotic part to this plea—one other men had played on.

It's clear to me now how ministers get themselves in foolish trouble. Someone in a bad marriage, in a particularly weak or insecure or otherwise vulnerable spot, could act on one of those occasions. And they do, more even than we hear about. Sam Wells is right to suggest that the double handshake is the right physical gesture with parishioners—plenty intimate, but not dangerously suggestive in the way even a hug can be. The deeper problem is the ennui, the sense of spiritual meaninglessness that would make such a tryst seem worthwhile. G. K. Chesterton is supposed to have said that the man appearing in church and the man knocking on the brothel door are looking for the same thing. The satisfaction of their deepest desire; in other words: God. Amazing how pathetically we sinners fall short.

But aside from the general sex-and-God connection, I'd like to think I cared about the sex lives of the elderly because the Bible cares about sex among the elderly. Withered Abram and Sarai are told they'll have a child; Sarai laughs, gets a name change to "Sarah," and salvation history lurches forward. "After I have grown old, and my husband is old, shall I have pleasure?" Sarah said, as one who both remembers such pleasure and remembers it in the distant past, where she'd just as soon it stay, thank you very much (Gen 18:12). Pleasure or not, God's going to get his baby, and his zillions more, in Israel and now in the church.

And now in old age the seniors of Beech Grove UMC want some company. And shame on me for assuming, even with some suggestion, that company would necessarily be sexual. Our age assumes that—for touch, for companionship to be meaningful it has to be genital. It's a decidedly thin view of intimacy that has simply to be wrong. Edith and Michael, their special friends and seasoned bodies, holding dried hands and tending awkward wounds over sweet tea on front porches in rural tobacco country in Zebulon County, North Carolina. Perhaps life is worth living, old age worth charging into. "I'm still here," Elizabeth said to me often. "Praise the Lord." The grumble in her voice made me wonder if she meant it. But spiritually she absolutely did—life is still good insofar as one has breath to praise the Lord. No new day is owed to us, so each is a gift. "Sometimes I wish I'd just go," Janet said to me once, "but then I realize I don't mean it." Indeed she doesn't. Old age is a crown of wisdom. The elderly made that church for me. They were my grandmothers and grandfathers aplenty. They were, are, beautiful. And they're still not gone. They never will be.

CHAPTER TWELVE

Divine Election

When I first arrived at Beech Grove as their full-time pastor, the community was bitterly divided. The problem was one member was running against another to be county commissioner. The primary issue in the election was whether to zone Beech Grove Road, on which sat Beech Grove Church. As you can imagine with zoning issues, questions of class weren't far behind: those in favor of zoning wanted progress, growth, economic opportunity, and their opponents were squirrel-eating backwoods rednecks. Those against zoning were for private ownership and the government butting out of their business—and their opponents were elitist Yankee know-it-alls. To make matters worse, the church member/candidate who was pro-zoning came from the church's old money family. The anti-zoning candidate came from the coarser stock of new money. One parishioner wise enough no longer to be attending church said to me "you got to understand, the Clintons were originally landowners, and the Landises were originally sharecroppers." Memories can outrun their usefulness. The Clintons were no longer wealthy; the Landises no longer poor. But words like *elitist* and *upstart* and *snob* and *white trash* have a way of lingering. As Faulkner said the past isn't dead, it's not even past.

So, as a Duke-trained theologian schooled in Stanley Hauerwas's Christian pacifism in which the church is the primary location of God's work in the world, what did I do? Well, I identified which side was going to lose the election, made friends with that side and subtly identified myself with them by taking their side in meetings over trivial things and accepting more of their dinner invitations, then isolated the headstrong advocate on the other side, befriended all his friends, left him on the outs socially, and when "my" side lost, I could commiserate more readily. The side that won didn't care, and in the end we only lost one family from the membership rolls. Sheer power politics, calculated not around the logic of the gospel, but around keeping a community together by being as cunning as possible. By the end we'd gained three families back and the church, eighty strong, grew by 10 percent in my time there, even built a building.

I basically preached one sermon while I was there. God loved us while we were yet enemies; how much more should we love our own enemies? Precisely there, among them, we meet the risen Christ. I wish I could say it's that sermon that "worked," but I think it was whatever personal skills I happened to have. To be crude about it, I may have learned more of what I needed to be a pastor at the fraternity house in college than in seminary; more from coming from a divorced family than from my church internships: how to build consensus, get people who don't necessarily like you to work with you, and keep meeting several times a week without killing one another.

This is no knock on theology. I prize what I learned at Duke. I'm tempted to say the more obscure the teaching there, the better. A systematician friend tells a story about a surly undergraduate who raised a hand during a lecture on the doctrine of the Trinity to say, "This is all irrelevant to me, I'm a marketing major. How could this ever help me to sell a taco?" My friend's answer: it won't, theology is useless. He meant that in the best sense. Theology is its own end: the praise of God. It's not meant to be used as an instrument for some higher good. I loved patristic Trinitarian debates precisely because they were useless—the "point" of the Trinity was to learn to contemplate God. The tacos will have to sell themselves.

Others who believe in doctrine and want it to be applicable to our ordinary lives have sought to stretch the former to cover the latter a bit. They call it "Social Trinitarianism," and reflect on the three persons as an ideal model for human persons in civic relationship. Here the Trinity often becomes an "argument" for democracy or egalitarianism. Now democracy is a fine thing, in doses (the problem with it, of course, is that you get the person whom most people want to be in charge. Most of the time.). But whatever else the Trinity "does," scoring points for democracy is not one of them.

Of course Social Trinitarianism was then and still is a popular way to talk about the Trinity in learned circles. As God is one and three, so the argument goes, we as church or body politic should also be united and plural. I have some sense this has declined in fashion as patristic scholars have cast doubt on whether patristic theologians themselves actually talked this way very much. The teaching also suggests a bit of bad faith. If you think the church should be more democratic, fine, say the church should be more democratic, but you don't have to raid the doctrine of the Trinity to do it. There may be *something* to it still—whatever identity and difference there is wholesomely understood among us is surely a reflection of the identity and difference that God already is. But I worry it doesn't tell us much. How was I to tell the Clintons and the Landises in Beech Grove Church to imitate the Trinity?

Lucky for me I didn't have to. *One* of the Trinity became incarnate and died, leaving us the pattern for how God would have us live. Not only that, but another of the Trinity is poured out on the church in Pentecost, sacraments, life together, to sweep us into the Triune life. The Trinity, in short, is not something "up there" we try and strain our gaze to look at and imitate, but something "down here," as it were, in Christ, in the church, straining us through enemy love into divine love. Augustine makes this point clear in *Confessions*—we strain our vision upward looking for God, and then stumble over the crucified slave at our feet. Maybe then theology isn't simply useless to church life, as it is with taco marketing, it's just *difficult* to relate to church life, as God is one to be adored and loved and not imitated at a distance.

But does the doctrine "argue" for the kind of power politics described above?

The Trinity doesn't tell the Clintons and the Landises how to live. It doesn't tell the rest of us who to vote for or how to keep a church from splitting. The Trinity says that One on the cross, raised three days later—that One is God, not less than the One who sent him. And that One who blows life through the church through history and through space and time now—that One is God, not less than the One on the cross who was raised three days later. How do we get along at election time? Who knows? Only the One who is Lord who will judge us all—even, or especially, when we think we're choosing our rulers.

I preached this one Trinity Sunday, using a famous quote from Augustine. Michael, my Hemingway-bearded old farmer, nodded in appreciation. "If you understand it, it is not God. I like it." It was the most theological word he ever said to me. And it came from the church itself insisting we cannot understand what the Triune nature *is*, let alone what to go and do about it. Now why exactly would a farmer like that so much, a note about how little we understand and how much less we can put our understanding to use? One who couldn't control when it would rain or what the market would do, but could work hard and pray for the best? It was *his* job to figure out what to go and *do* because of the Triune life among us. I just preached the lectionary text that the church served up for that Sunday.

I was struck during that zoning controversy how little I did to keep the church together. The ones really leading were the old ladies—molasses-sweet, blue-haired, Bible-believing old ladies who attended our Wednesday night prayer meeting.

The dispute did hurt our church terribly. Longtime members threatened to leave, or at least resign leadership posts (which they left effectively vacant anyway). People worried openly about a church split. In one Administrative Board meeting I found myself with one candidate and his spouse, and the campaign manager of the other and his spouse. The two men had once been close friends. Their sons still were. They'd known each other since their baptisms. Their parents still talked about how wonderful the other's grandparents were. And their dispute wasn't nearly as nasty or personal as that between their wives. The two couples were not even speaking (thankfully, perhaps). Yet we were to pass a budget together? The most painful part was that they were all good people who still knew how to get their hands dirty and fix a motor, prepare a casserole, and teach a Sunday school lesson, and in their business lives they could balance a million-dollar budget. But could not, for the life of them (or their pastor), get along.

And precisely there is the small church's glory. You can't avoid the person you hate. You can't wiggle out of the meeting with the person you're not speaking to. And because of it you have a shot at being Christian.

Amidst the tumult I had to deal with "prayer meetin'," as we North Carolinians call it. When I first became pastor and heard such a meeting existed I was primed to kill it. I'd insist on having communion each time it met, or be otherwise engaged every Wednesday night, or something, anything, to avoid a Baptist-style "sweet hour of prayer." And Baptist it was—every member had been a Baptist at some point (this is common among Methodists in the rural South). Some left when a Baptist church exploded, or over a dispute with a pastor, or whatever. They were (mostly) glad for Methodist polity in which a bishop can step into a church fight and impose order, as they had all seen Baptist churches dash themselves against the rocks. Though, occasionally, they were none too happy with where they heard their tithes were going. When the United Methodists made sympathetic noises about gay people or pacifists, they fumed. "Why don't we go independent?" one asked me. Wait—weren't you the one who saw the Baptist church run that poor family out for music or lipstick or misinterpretation of Leviticus? They never meant it.

But they did long for that ole-time religion. One would often tell me of a traveling evangelist troupe of some sort that had come through the county decades before. Ellen regaled me this way: "They had people down the aisles at the altar call, crying, repenting. My husband and I got saved that night." Then she would look at me with a mischievous gleam, "We could have that here you know, if we prayed hard enough."

If someone was sick the prayer meetin' would anoint them. If someone not present was sick they'd anoint someone present as a proxy on the ill person's behalf. One night one proudly displayed a rock she'd been given at a conference. It had a Star of David on it. "The speaker gave it to us as a reminder that anyone who blesses Israel will be blessed, and if America doesn't bless Israel, we'll be cursed" (they only *thought* they didn't like sacraments—but they adored their own physical places where God meets us). Another asked me once whether, when the Rapture comes, it'll be China that invades the United States, since she heard they had the biggest army in the world. Courageous Bible teacher that I was, I told her the North Koreans actually have a bigger army.

One Sunday a visitor stood up during service and began shouting. The Lord is going to burn this world up with fire! We better be ready! We need the gifts of the Holy Ghost! We waited for him to stop and leave. One of my prayer ladies on her way out of church said to me, "Did you hear him? He says he told us what the Holy Ghost told him to. And I believe him!"

One of the prayer meetin' ladies didn't care for all the screaming. "That was real ugly the way he did that. He should shout at his own church if he wants to carry on that way."

I told her he handed me $100 on his way out. "He said it was a gift from the Holy Ghost."

"He did?" she asked, two or three syllables on "did." She thought a minute. "Well, that was real nice of him, wasn't it? Did you tell him he could come back?"

I found myself going to prayer meetin', and wishing for its success, because we sure needed prayer, especially then. I could hardly have a conversation with anyone in the community, church member or not, in which the election didn't come up. Can you believe what Clinton said? Have you heard what Landis did? How can a Christian act that way? Do you know his daddy has money and wants this zoning to make more of it? They had a meeting the other night and they was cussin' and drinkin'—can you believe it? They expect me to go to church with those people? And so on.

In fact, the only people who didn't talk about the election incessantly were the prayer ladies. That's because they were talking about Jesus incessantly, and getting people saved, and healing sick people, and making America more Christian (I'm for these all, even the last, though it meant something different to me). When politics came up in prayer meetin', no one was shocked. These women had been through a lot of life, not all of it pretty. They had buried family members and spouses and friends, seen prodigal sons and daughters wander off and never return. That's precisely why they prayed so hard. So they weren't surprised or aghast at what people are capable of doing. They'd seen it all before. They just "lifted it up to the Lord," as they liked to say, letting it weigh on Jesus' shoulders instead of their own.

This isn't to say the prayer ladies didn't have opinions on the election. I could've told you who supported whom, who felt like who was being un-Christian, whose husband fished with whose daddy and so had the couple's vote. But here's the key: this wasn't the most important thing about them. It wasn't even on the list of the top ten most important things about them. It was just another item on the prayer list: that the church wouldn't be hurt, that souls wouldn't be twisted by the political finagling, that joy in denouncing someone else wouldn't turn into that worst of all sins—pride. They'd seen it happen with the Baptists, they didn't think it could with the Methodists, but an even more important glue for holding the church together than a bishop was prayer meetin'.

Their example encouraged me. More than that, they got after me. If I hinted that Scripture wasn't as historically reliable as they liked, they let me know about it. If I started doubting that God could do miracles, they set me straight. There was a toughness there that made you quiver if you ran afoul of it. One, who sang in the choir, noticed the choir member behind her wasn't joining in to sing "Praise God" at the right moment. So during the choir's Sunday performance, decked out in blue robes and leading us all in song, she turned around at the right instant and barked at her colleague, "Praise God," with a scowl on her face that signaled she meant it. It is right to praise God. Now shape up.

Once I tried to defer pastoral authority on some decision or other in the passive-aggressive hope that someone else would make the hard decision. I joked, "Don't ask me, I only work here." My beloved Mamie came right back: "No you don't, you *lead* here."

Heartened by their example and given ballast by their support, I started praying for our elected leaders in Sunday service, as Christians have always done (even when those leaders were feeding them to lions). I prayed over the election and asked that we would witness to our faith in public in this and in all our lives. Lo and behold, the nineth chapter of Romans came up in the lectionary, with its description of God's "election" of us in Christ. My sermon title that Sunday was "The Election." I opened, "No, not that one." And preached that there is another election far more important than this one, which only seemed important. Encouraged by the prayer ladies, our "biggest crisis" was set in perspective. November would come and go, the church would be here another hundred years to bury these candidates' grandchildren, as long as someone was praying on Wednesday night.

One of them noticed I preached a much more Wesleyan sermon not long after, insisting we are free to respond to God's mercy with repentance . . . or not.

"Isn't that different than what you said about election before?" he asked.

"Yes, but this biblical text said something different," I said, hoping he wouldn't accuse me of saying the Bible disagreed with itself.

"Got it," he responded, satisfied I was just being biblical, not confusing, before heading home to collard greens.

Those elder pray-ers were Beech Grove's most genuine leaders. People didn't come to church for the preaching or the programming or the music. They came because of those women. When one told you she was praying for you it meant something. When one hugged you, you remembered all week. When one cooked for you the casserole tasted like someone loved you. And when you were around them you were in the presence of Jesus. Their presence, their dogged refusal to let the church be merely political, kept the church's fabric from pulling apart at the seams. We were about Jesus, after all, not anything so parochial as a county board election (can someone tell this to the presidential candidates every four years, please?). And the way to stay about Jesus was to forgive like Jesus forgives, to treat enemies like God does—with kindness.

The election didn't turn out well for Clinton, the incumbent. He was viewed as too tied in to moneyed interests in the county who stood to gain by the road's zoning, and was voted out handily. Landis had some missteps early in his commissionership, which Clinton reveled in. In short, the election didn't go away. When we argued about whether and how to build a new parsonage the argument fell along "party lines." All of Clinton's people were for it; Landis's were against it. What did the parsonage have to do with the election? Nothing at all (except something vague about the zoners wanting progress and the non-zoners liking the way things were). The grooves in the road were well worn by then, we just kept barreling along with them.

Except eventually the election did fade from our consciousness. Not because its effects vanished, as I say. But because the church remembered its first job was to be the church, not a partisan entity. That both Clinton and Landis and all their friends and kin belonged there and none would be kicked out for doing something they shouldn't. That the prayer ladies were right: when things are bad, pray. Then pray again. Pray harder. Then pray some more. And "praise God!" already. Do that, and the church will redirect itself toward Jesus and away from its own pettiness. So we were transformed, at least a little, slowly, and with difficulty. But we were.

Candidate Clinton later told me of something that happened in church quite against his will. During the passing of the peace, directly before the communion liturgy, he found himself face to face with candidate Landis (God bless the small church!). Instead of frowning or turning away, he reached out his hand. "I couldn't believe I did that," he said. "But if there's anyplace where we should be friends, it's right there, before the Lord's Supper."

That's the church at its best: forgiving before it knows what it's doing, erring on the side of grace even when we'd rather not.

It was a slow transformation, not a miraculous reconciliation. After the election some folks drifted away even more, never returning to their leadership posts in the parish. They've not joined other churches, they're just in the etherlike netherworld of not-quite-in-my church (what's the joke about the Baptists stranded on the desert island who built two churches—one was his, one was the one he *used* to go to? There'll always be people who *used to go* to Beech Grove. The "church alumni club," someone called it.). I'm sure the scars remain for the active political participants. But everyone else realized we were a people of prayer, not partisanship. They continued reaching out to those who weren't around as much anymore, trying to lure them back. The church has even gained some new members since I left, which suggests a health and vitality that were never lost, only threatened. The church survived and will continue to. The credit, such as it is, goes not to my successor, the new young whippersnapper pastor being kept in line (I actually found myself thinking—just how young *is* she?). It goes to the prayer ladies who're helping her mind her Bible and reminding her to come to prayer meetin'.

Churches like The United Methodist are only as good as these small parishes. And these parishes are only as good as the old ladies' prayer meetings. In a sense then, the whole church rests on shoulders such as theirs. Good thing they're hunched in prayer.

CHAPTER THIRTEEN

How to Talk Right

The people of Zebulon have the oddest Southern accent I know. They pronounce a few vowels like Canadians. "Let's go on out to the huse," Mamie said to me at one point. It's almost like it needs a German umlaut, "hös," a vowel that starts low and ends scraping grass roots. "The fäther is usually like the son, isn't he?" one asked, again, strikingly Canadian-like. "Fauwther," almost, a vowel only the Germans make. Weird.

Their ancestors weren't the best spellers. Jaylynn's church and town, Buelah, are named for an almost unbearable old-timey gospel hymn:

> O Beulah land, sweet Beulah land!
> As on thy highest mount I stand,
> I look away across the sea
> Where mansions are prepared for me
> And view the shining glory shore
> My heaven, my home forever more.

The text the song comes from is glorious: Isaiah's promise that Israel shall no longer be Desolate, but shall be called (in the original King Jimmy), Beulah, or, translated, "married." Only they couldn't spell so well. So it became Buelah, a more Spanish-sounding rendering of a King James verse.

Now *that's* a way to name a town. Far better a long-forgotten verse in prophecy than for a wealthy benefactor or the wrong bunch of trees or someplace in England.

A former pastor of Jaylynn's church used to say "they're doing badly at Buelah and they need rehab at Rehobeth." It was gallows humor, but it was about right.

Zebulon Countyers also have their own linguistic constructions as every region does: to give someone a ride is to "carry" them someplace. A "homeplace" is the house one grew up in, as opposed to a mere home or a house (these may be more generically Southern and rural and not exclusive to Zebulon, but bear with me). Once in a sermon I thought I'd go native: "Jesus comes to carry us to a new homeplace." They smiled and nodded—as exuberant as white churches get. I'd bothered to notice their language.

I wonder now how often they actually liked my jokes, stories, sermons, anything. In fact, I squirm to think of how many bad ones they sat through. Patiently. Lovingly. One member told me that my successor, "has been great, just like you were great. We've been so blessed." I'm just not sure how great we Methodist ministers are. Our people certainly are, not least for bearing with us.

Consider the church service on a recent trip back—one of my first in that building as a pure observer, no pastoral role at all. An enormous mural of Jesus presides over proceedings from behind the pulpit. It's at least eight feet tall, easily some twelve feet wide. It depicts Jesus praying in Gethsemane. His image is not too interesting—bearded, mildly Semitic, looking toward gleaming upward light, influenced undoubtedly by Warner Sallman's soulless *Head of Christ*, which sits in countless rural churches in this country. What impressed me in this case is the background: dark, foreboding, terrifying almost. Three quivering, plotting disciples are silhouetted just behind him. There is no hint of the redemption on the other side of this cross. Just darkness. However mindlessly chipper our singing might become, that dark backdrop suggests something wise about life— it may be more dark than light. But Jesus will be there.

All that is going on right behind the preacher's head. I couldn't help looking at it as Alexis preached, pacing back and forth as she did. Sometimes I could see Jesus, sometimes I couldn't, and this was in no way coordinated with the new pastor's success or lack of it that Sunday. It just correlates with her pacing schedule.

Now you see Jesus, now you don't: it's a perfect image for preaching. Sometimes the preacher gets out of the way and lets the people see Jesus. Sometimes we block him. Sometimes we pace back and forth, alternately letting him shine and letting ourselves. I noticed the new pastor moved around a lot—I could mostly see Jesus. I stood still for two full years in that pulpit. Who did I block—*that entire time?*

The choir, blue-robed, seriously visaged, paces in during the processional. They sing to canned music, with gusto. People even sing solo. *Solo.* Singing out loud in front of dozens of peers. Men and women both. It amazes me to think what bravery is required to sing this way, and how much more to participate in that choir (I declined, as humiliation is not high on my to-do list). If you want classical choral excellence, head elsewhere. If you want lovers of Jesus singing about him in front of friends and strangers and all, come here. You know my vote for which is more beautiful.

Lauren Winner likes to ask where in our culture do people make music together. When do pagans sing? After the national anthem at football games and "Happy Birthday," the list grows short. Where do you find song that's offered not because the singer puts on a worthy show, but because she prays a heartfelt prayer? Not because we're trying to win some sort of competition, but just for the goodness of music, or the goodness of God? Human beings thrive as they sing—

we do irreligious neighbors no favor by not inviting them to church to sing with us. Excellence is beside the point. The small church makes that connection unmistakable.

As I watched my successor I wondered how often I did similar things—made mistakes and covered them with corny jokes ("it's sure hard not to hit that microphone and make it squeal, isn't it?"), told children's sermons without point, droned past several good sermon endings. What skill it takes to bear with the church. To tolerate ministers such as we, singers like us.

And think of all the rest of it—the church asks for your money, your time, your cooking, your volunteering hours, your cheerfulness, your butt in the pew. These treasures are not easily given up. Especially when the guy in the pew next to you is, well, not the best neighbor. "Maxie Hillman," one man introduced himself to me, as though I hadn't shaken his hand every Sunday for two years, and known him even before that. When I'd first met their family I complimented him to another member. "He seems like a great guy." She looked at me quizzically. "His wife is a saint." If you can't say anything nice . . .

Whoever your worst enemy is, she or he will be there in the pew beside you. It's the law of the church. We attract dysfunctional people even more than most human organizations. Only we can't easily keep anybody out or remove people once they're there. We open the doors, half beg people to come, and when they do, even if they're annoying, we let them in. Those without plentiful social outlets—they especially—are there every time we open the doors. Church growth literature works largely because amidst thousands of worshipers you can ignore such people. In a room of fifty you can't. There they are. And if you want to meet Jesus, you've got to go through them. Which is handy—Jesus meets us in the form of our worst enemies.[1] Our efforts to love them may bring about their conversion or an unexected friendship. But usually not. We should pay attention to that irritation, that lack of comfort. For that person is an image bearer of the living God, a brother or sister of Jesus himself, one in whom the Holy Spirit rumbles. We should bow, genuflect, as Archbishop Desmond Tutu says, at any meeting with any other person. That's an image of the invisible God. She looks like Jesus. Even if she bugs the bejesus out of us.

That's church attendance at the small church: it's a sort of suffering through, a matter of bearing one's cross, not unlike anything difficult and worth doing, from athletic training to marriage to university education. An *askesis*, we call it in academic circles—a way of training your body and soul to align properly with God's will. It requires a sort of death to self. It's dark up there on that mural. You learn to bear with the preacher. With the worship. With one another. It's incredibly difficult. And just so, going through it, you become more like Jesus. And having conformed to him, we hang on to him as he rises.

---

1. I take this argument from Rowan Williams's *Resurrection: Interpreting the Easter Gospel* (Cleveland: Pilgrim Press, 2003).

CHAPTER FOURTEEN

A Pharaoh Who
Knew Not Joseph

How much of our lives is controlled by wealthy people whom we cannot see?

This was not only the case in the 2008 economic meltdown, when local banks sold mortgages to God-knows-who across the globe (I fear this will be remembered as the mistake of lending money to poor people; when it was just as much the mistake of lending money to rich people). For me it was the case in sales during a summer job in college. I was to peddle phone book advertising to local businesses in Boston. Little did I know that whole city blocks would be owned by a single person who would either squeeze the trigger on a sale or not. Let's call this species of creature a PIM (Powerful, Invisible Man). Such invisible, powerful owners in Boston wouldn't even let me in to see them. Sales taught me a lot that helps in ministry—how to chat people up, put them at ease, get them to do what you want (both sales and ministry have a component of manipulation—hopefully the latter to a godly end). Mostly they taught me to be kind to the people who leave messages for you. "That asshole called again" is a far cry different from "I had the most wonderful chat with this lovely young pastor today—you should call him back." But as to cracking the door of the boss in Boston who had it bolted—no.

The same held true in Zebulon. There was a powerful old money family with a PIM patriarch named Earn (short for Earnest, I reckon) who owned gobs of land around the church. He and his family were partly behind the zoning fight, for they could see the future in rural North Carolina lay not with textiles or tobacco or furniture—pretty soon those things will be made or manufactured no closer than China. Whatever economic future lay in making the place a bedroom community. So they wanted to get to work developing their unused land

and selling it at a pretty penny to people working in Greensboro, the Triangle, or points farther afield. By the time I left they had houses up and selling at Chicago-like prices—and they looked like they merited it. They were gorgeous. The other church members were right to think we should attract some of those new families. Some probably came eventually. I was more sanguine. People in houses like the Chicago suburbs probably want Willow Creek-style worship, with a polished show and no commitments necessary. It's probably unfair of me to assume such a hole in their souls. God can make any bones to live. But those fields didn't look white for harvest to me.

So this PIM was parceling out his land, bulldozing trees for houses, making things move at the county level. He was also kin to the Landises, then at the throats of the Clintons (and vice versa), in our church. They were some sort of cousins once removed, or married to a second cousin, in some combination perhaps opaque even to them. They only came to church occasionally, and then without much enthusiasm. The only other time I ever saw him was as he sat in his front yard, waving to passing cars by a pile of wood that, perhaps, he was thinking of chopping one day. I'd wave back, knowing he wouldn't likely be there Sunday. But his specter was there all the same. One night an ordinary parsonage meeting turned into an odd referendum on this PIM, on local politics, and then on me.

Everything was a go on the parsonage. The land was ready and cleared. The county had given us our building permit. One of our myriad of handy parishioners had designed and was going to build the thing. I could see an argument against having someone in-house build for you. If it goes wrong, you lose a parishioner. And you can't exactly yell at the builder when he gets behind schedule. But I'd have trusted Jimmy with my life, much more with building a building of which he and the church would be proud. With the way his family gave, he was all but paying for it anyway.

"Earn says the house will be too close to the road," someone announced. I blanched. The PIM had spoken in the meeting, even if through a proxy. Not that he responded to my request that he be on this committee. He could own it with just a word, spoken after months of our meeting together. I'd laid eyes on him only half a dozen times and here he was vouching for control of my life.

"Why? Who's he think he is? Telling us what to do?" someone from the other side asked.

Turns out our future parsonage was near enough to his exurban mansions that he wanted a say in how it looked. He wasn't making a suggestion. His command was defended with worries that being too close to the road would endanger future parsonage-dwelling children. But mostly he wanted it set back, like his mansions, at an austere, suitable distance from the asphalt.

The PIM had spoken. Smoke was coming from behind the curtain.

"He's a powerful man. He's been good to this church," someone said, reminding that he had sold the parsonage land to us at a discount, or cleared it for us, or some other such favor, the cost of which to him had been minimal, but had indeed helped us.

"It's just like county government, him up in everybody else's business," another responded.

I was nervous. "I think we should be aware he could sue us to make this happen," I said. I had no idea what I was talking about. I mean, I thought he could sue us, though it'd be odd for a man to sue his own church. But I was more pointing to the PIM syndrome. Someone else was making us dance, calling the tune even, and I didn't care for it. Didn't he know how important this was to my ministry? Uh, I mean to the church's future?

"Jason!" one of his supporters exclaimed. "I can't believe you! Why would you say that about a good man in our community?" Actually, she wasn't a huge supporter of Earn's, she just disliked the people in the church who disliked him, and now she was into me. Her husband tried to catch her eye, shaking his head, but she was having none of it. "That's quite a nasty thing to say about somebody, and you being a preacher, I can't believe you!" I had said nastier things in private about the PIM, but never publicly, and she was giving me more-than-public hell about it. I flushed. She wouldn't stop. "I expect better from you."

There were no good options. Either we leapt, and so looked like we were at the beck and call of the PIM, much to the chagrin of the Clinton supporters who already loathed the guy. Then I'd look like I was in the pocket of that faction, to the detriment of my relationship with the others. Or we refused, and the happy and angry parties would swap, and the PIM could likely make our lives miserable in other ways. I mentioned a lawsuit, but was afraid there were other things a PIM could do in a rural county that I had no idea about. Was it always this hot in here?

"Jimmy, can we do this without changing the plans?" someone asked wisely, turning to the expertise of the future builder. Jimmy was respected on all sides. Even I had no idea whose side he was on politically. And perhaps just so when he spoke he could use his whisper. Everybody listened intently.

"Yeah, I reckon could. Might even be better. The onliest problem is it'll take a little more brick in the back—the incline is sharper there—but we can do it. Won't even need to change the per*mit*." The accent was always on the second syllable of that word, per*mit*. I loved the way he, they, used the word *onliest*, as though *only* needed a superlative form. That way of saying per*mit* had a certain authority to it.

Such words had never sounded more beautiful.

Everyone calmed down. The tension had gone out of the room. "Jimmy, you're a genius!" I told him later. He shrugged. "You catch more flies with honey than vinegar," he said.

It is on the shoulders of men and women like Jimmy that small churches are built. People bigger than petty politics, bigger than pastors' egos, able to take the heat out of a fight with just a word. He didn't even shift position in the chair he leaned back in or take his toothpick out. Anybody left who wanted to fight would have to find some other issues to do it over.

My assailant in the meeting never apologized. She didn't have to. She'd detected that my comment was more about my getting what I wanted professionally, at the expense of a PIM's reputation in church members' eyes, than on the mission of the church in that place. She was against me in a way that was for me.

As for how to deal with a PIM in a local church (or elsewhere)? I still have no idea. But we didn't let him have the last word in that meeting or between us as church members. He might've been kin to some present in that room, or a hated, Wizard-of-Oz figure to others (like me). But because of Jimmy our baptism mattered more that night than our blood. Occasionally this church stuff all works out.

CHAPTER FIFTEEN

An Arena
for Holiness

One man who had the worst time bearing with me was named Bob. Not because he isn't kind. He's big-hearted, neighborly, like molasses—sweet and solid. He patted me on the back and congratulated me on not losing my Southern accent on that trip back after I'd moved away. "They didn't turn you Yankee, did they?" Bob is a former Baptist, like most of my best parishioners. He got saved during a traumatic robbery experience at a truck stop. He likes his Bible straight, his Jesus unadulterated, and his politics decidedly right of center. All of this was fine. Until the war came around.

He didn't say much the first time I preached against the 2003 Iraq War. He'd learned well to hold his tongue if you had nothing nice to say. He just told me how much he liked Charles Stanley's sermon he'd heard on the radio in the run up to the war. Stanley had accused war protestors of being enemy agents, friends of terrorists, amidst his general blessing of weapons and flag. I nodded, took his meaning, and moved on.

I didn't mean to preach against war again. I just couldn't help it—the lectionary's gospel lesson was "get behind me satan," a refusal of conquistador messiahship and embrace of suffering servanthood (see Mark 8:31-38). What a contrast, I said, to America's warlike ways (I told you they had a lot to put up with from me!).

This was enough for Bob. "I had enough of this . . . mess," he said, controlling himself to avoid emitting the only cussword I would ever hear him almost say (his slate is still clean). "You said all this before. I listened. And I had enough. You talk about the Bible and stay out of my politics." I nodded, sulked, and returned to a ruined day.

What'd I expect him to say? What did I expect the church members to do? Take to the streets and protest? Write their legislator? Not send their kids to war? They'd found ways to agree with me the first time I'd preached—war is hell, they agreed, no one should relish it, it's a terrible duty. One man mentioned his dad came back from being mustard gassed in World War I a mean old drunk, beating the kids. Another told me how glad he was to avoid going to Vietnam by way of his Navy service. "I could have been in one of them awful gunboats," he said. None of them denounced war generally, as I took Jesus to have done and told them they should do. They bore with me insofar as they could. Amen'd. Softly.

Second time around Bob had enough. The first time he just told me to listen to Reverend Stanley. The second time Bob stormed out. Stomped off. Made threats of discontinuing his pledge (a genuine disaster. God bless the Baptists. They teach their people to tithe.).

This saddened me for more than just ecclesial reasons. I loved Bob. He sang in the choir. He married a divorcée with several children to raise on her own, and was a good husband and stepdad to the kids after they'd had it rough. He came every Sunday. He was a dream of a churchman (did I bless the Baptists yet?).

He was also an amateur racecar driver. Every Saturday he'd race at South Boston Speedway, forty or fifty laps, in a car he'd made himself with his buddies. He'd grown up dragging around unpaved roads in rural southwestern Virginia. Raising hell, clearly, he told me in as many words. All this preconversion. But Jesus didn't take away his love of racing. If anything, he enhanced it. "I win a race," he said, "and there's more money in the plate the next day—I got winnings to tithe against." So we prayed for him of course, and not just for his health. "Some say you should tithe what you clear, but I think it ought to be against what you gross." Can we clone this man?

You can see why losing him would be a disaster for the church. He loved Jesus enough that a split with his church would be a split in his own soul too. How do we preachers manage to run off people so in love with God?

He wasn't the only one unhappy. Ashley, my most beloved parishioner, the one who'd stay by me more than anyone else, tried to get at her unhappiness by indirection. "I hear The Methodist Church is funneling money to the war protestors," she said. "That's my money given to God in the plate going to something I hate." At least that one was easy enough. Our various general boards had denounced the war, sure enough, to their credit (as is more clear now, and should have been then). But they hardly had cash to dole out to leftover hippies, as Ashley feared. Isn't it amazing how much of this is a rehash of Vietnam-era stereotypes? The violence-hungry marine killing children; the pot-smoking hairy lefty? At least the minister can make a few calls and clear up a Limbaugh-inspired misperception.

Early that next week I went to Bob's garage, where he polished and worked on and souped up his vehicle. "So it's a Chrysler?" I asked, noting the logo. "Nah, buddies and I built this car," he said. "From spare parts. The bottom up. Before computers I could do this," he lamented. "But I couldn't build one now. Cars all run on computers. I can't work a computer." He said this as though it were a defeat. "All I can make is an automobile from the ground up." Astonishing.

I couldn't convince him of my biblicism, love for Jesus, or anything else. I was just a liberal, he explained, nicely as he could. He didn't trust me now, after the second antiwar sermon. I'd chosen the Democrats over worship (never mind that Democrats were beating the war drum as loudly as W. at that point). I should expect him to keep his distance.

Lucky for me, for us, his churchmanship was more resilient than that.

And, lucky for me, his mother-in-law died. Not lucky for anyone else, of course. She was a marvelous woman. Very sick for a very long time. Her death was tragic, as every death is.

And it was exactly what I needed.

I loaded up for this funeral. Practiced, memorized, got good stories, souped them up a little (as we all want done for us) and let it rip on funeral day. It's a good day, anyway, to be on one's A-game, preachingwise: the building is full, everyone's dressed up. They want a good word. And I had one.

Afterward, Bob introduced me to some of his old Baptist friends, including a minister. "Yeah, my preacher done good today, didn't he?" he beamed, proud, banging me on the back like an old pal. This was the only way to earn his trust back: to preach the word. It's the only "weapon" a preacher should wish to wield to achieve that end (2 Cor 10:4). A few weeks later I let one rip on John 3:16, had an altar call, brought out the works again. "Nice to hear the gospel preached every now and again," he joked, winking at me. I laughed back. It hurt. But in a good way.

Mainline churches have often not had a place for people like Bob: blue-collar, conservative, rough around the edges, willing to challenge a biblical interpretation he sees as wrong. But really we're only as good as we are like him. Not for the conservatism necessarily, not even for the salt-of-the-earth ordinariness, but for the biblicism, the love for Jesus, the stalwart support of the church. Even for the willingness to get up into a preacher's face if necessary. Without that, we're nothing.

CHAPTER SIXTEEN

No One's Cute Up Close

Zebulon's county seat of Bartlett looks, if anything, more depressed than the little "communities" our churches were in. The only car dealer is gone. You can lease that property cheaply now if you want. One of the two pizza places is gone. Food Lion, a Southern chain grocer, and McDonald's are still there. One would think restaurants would have a future. People gotta eat. But it doesn't look to be growing. No wonder the kids of Zebulon County tend to leave.

There are two stoplights in town. They're called the old and the new stoplight. The old one is decades old. The new one, well, years old. There's a lovely restored county courthouse on the main square, refurbished at a pretty penny recently enough ago that folks still complained about it. There's a few antique stores down there, an abandoned movie theater still used for nothing else, and some more places to eat. One was once owned by an Egyptian. In the days after 9/11, he plastered his place with Americana. It didn't matter. A de facto boycott was on. He closed. Who could be more pro-Western and pro-capitalism than an Egyptian refugee come to America to start a business, and in rural North Carolina of all places? Didn't matter. He was the wrong religion and color. And he was gone. It's a steak place now.

Zebulon County is where people get a speeding ticket on their way between the University of North Carolina and Virginia Tech. Got to keep the county in business somehow. If people don't remember that they remember the Hardee's. Got to pee somewhere en route to Hokie country. The county commissioners have dreams of the place becoming a tech corridor, or the aforementioned bed-room community. They're grasping at straws. But I don't blame them. What else can the place produce, post tobacco?

Jerry worked for the federal government in tobacco inspection for his whole career. The bulk of his job was travel. The FDA would fly him out of North Carolina to India or China, where he was to direct local growers in growing tobacco. "I knew I was putting places like Zebulon County out of business," he said. "Their leaf was terrible. But it was just a matter of time before you could smoke it." And now Europe and Asia do. No wonder he didn't care for the very fed'ral gub'ment he worked decades for.

Here's the funny part—how, amidst all that, did he get to be as gentle as the landscape whose economic livelihood he was directed to root up?

The hills there are placid, getting up toward rolling in a procession that ends in the Smoky Mountains. If you go just a little north and west the hills get big and turn blue and the banjos come out. There'd be good sledding if there was snow that stuck around. There's great hunting and fishing and hiking.

It's rural enough that the Amish have taken up residence there. They lived on our same road, technically in Branch, North Carolina (*used to* have a post office. That building is now New Testament Fire-Baptized Church. Branch has almost as many churches as residents). They ran an Amish country store. Our parishioners accused the Amish store owners of buying in bulk at Walmart and replacing the labels with Amish cuteness. Maybe they did, but whether or not, it was expensive enough. I told the man there who introduced himself as "Yoder" that I studied in seminary a great Mennonite theologian named John Howard Yoder who taught at Notre Dame. Mr. Yoder just looked at me like I might bite him. The Amish store is now opening a new, bigger branch in one of the abandoned spaces closer to Bartlett. During a time when everything else is closing.

The Amish presence meant the local grocery store still had a hitching post while we lived there. When I got in a traffic accident nearby once, the state trooper told me, "Lordy, I was worried, I heard I was going to Branch Road and thought I'd have a mess of a horse to clean up." Parishioners joked about how the Amish smelled (they go for the natural odor thing) and how they dressed (which I thought one of their better traits). They didn't know as much about how they pastored—though the world would come to learn more after the Amish school shooting in Pennsylvania some years after.

Once a young, bonneted Amish woman came and sat down in our parsonage. She looked around. "Man," she said. "Your house is really *small!*" It hurts to be pitied by the Amish. We came to find out that Amish may be plain people, unlike us "English," as they still call us, but their homes are big. That's where they worship, so the space has to be as big as our sanctuaries. And where they raise their dozen or more kids. Our parsonage, designed for a nice, mid-century Methodist minister family with no more than two kids, was indeed tiny to her. So would most local living rooms seem. How much did she get out?

We'd heard of her through the Zebulon Parish office—a conglomerate of church offices banded together to run a thrift store, print bulletins, and generally take a load off of area churches. We got a call that a young Amish girl needed some pastoral care, preferably from a woman. Jaylynn was the only woman pastor in the county. This was particularly fun at the Gideons' annual fund-raiser. There was a plant on the table for all the "wives." I took one. Seemed like I qualified. Anyway, there was one woman pastor within shouting distance, ergo, over the Amish girl came.

We were curious—what could this be about? But mostly we were excited to have a conversation with one of the Amish people. Suddenly they weren't exotic, cute, in bonnets, with buggies. She was a human being, making jokes, at our expense, and with pastoral problems she brought to us that really only God could solve.

Turns out she had problems with her pastor's wife. Here she was, young but not a girl, certainly past the age where she could have married. And she was unmarried. She was also struggling with her vocation. Should she stay with the Amish or move on? She could leave, as others had done, go to college, make a different sort of life. But that'd be breaking bridges she might later want to cross. She loved Jesus, loved her church, and didn't want to leave all that. What should she do?

She and Jaylynn met in private, of course, about whatever other matters I'm not sure. And away she went. We didn't hear from her again, until she'd decided to leave. Not the church, but the community. "There are other communities in Kentucky; I think I'll go join them," she said. She'd taken her earnings from Yoder's store and bought a new Dodge Viper (now it was, once again, time for us to envy her material goods). She'd packed it up and was going. "I just wanted to thank you for helping me," she said. It had been entirely our pleasure.

The Amish aren't cute, up close. They're just people. They're also not malicious interlopers, as the gossip about them would have—reselling Walmart products and all. They just work hard, are thrifty, and succeed financially. But their churches fracture easily. Their commitment to a forgotten way of life doesn't preclude the sort of mobility that breaks up communities and leaves us stuck in individualism that the rest of us in modernity face, as the young woman's story shows.

Getting to know one Amish woman, just a little, showed me the danger of patronizing country people generally. Books like this that sing the praises of small church or otherwise rural ministry run the risk of suggesting country people are cute, ministry there is languid but satisfying, that life is filled with sweet tea and slaps on the back. It is not so. It is difficult to live in such places oftentimes. Their schools struggle. Kids who don't hunt and fish are bored. Bored kids try out meth in addition to youth group. Lonely people act in strange ways. Schools struggle to educate kids well. And generally the pews are filled with odd people who wouldn't fit in anywhere else.

The reason to love them is that they are creatures made in God's image and redeemed by Christ, being wooed by the power of the Spirit into life in the church, where we live in love with God and God's whole creation. That is, the same reasons everyone else on planet earth is lovable.

Not because they're cute.

CHAPTER SEVENTEEN

Discipleship Despite Sunday School

Sunday school was not my favorite time of the week. As in any church it's hard to get people to fill the Sunday school teaching posts. Until they do—and then it's hard to get them out. One man told me he'd led his class for ten years. "Wow, that's great!" I said. Until I visited the class. It was the "young adults' class," without a participant under forty (I've heard of classes with the name whose youngest member is not under seventy). Lester would sit down on his comforter in front of the TV Saturday night and pray over what to say. He'd be led to something. And then his Bible index became his handiest teaching tool. He'd look up all the verses for the topic of the day—say, "empowerment" or "Spirit" or "Rapture" or "speaking in tongues" (are you noticing a pattern?). The class would saunter in, start ten or fifteen minutes late, begin with inside jokes even I wasn't privy to, and then Lester would read the verses pertaining to his topic. He'd usually circle things back around to a variant on this theme: "You probably can't be a good Christian without being a good American, and it's probably true the other way around too." Not that he knew any non-Americans or non-Christians, or really any bad Americans or Christians, except on television. I don't mean this to suggest Lester was ungracious in his manner about leading his class. He was quick to admit the Bible index was his best—or even only—teaching tool. And he'd have handed the class off if someone else wanted. It's just to say the young adults' class had a certain . . . formulaic quality to it. They never did ask me to teach.

To prepare for another young adults' I had to study up on the book of Colossians. In one moment we were marveling over the cosmic scope of the book's language for Jesus: "He is the image of the invisible God, the firstborn of all creation" (1:15).

"Isn't that beautiful?" I asked.

"Yeah, but what's it mean?"

"Sorry?"

"The image of the invisible God."

"Right, beautiful isn't it?"

"How can you have an image of something invisible?"

Silence. Who let the smart laypeople in? She was not only smart, she was tough as nails—raising a disabled daughter as a single mom, leading all the church's music. The church rallied around her and her daughter, building a ramp, cherishing the girl whenever she was present, asking after her when she was away. Now here her mom was, wanting an answer to a serious theological question, and I had none. What did I go to seminary for, again?

"I mean, if you took a picture of a soul or a ghost, nothing would show up—it's something invisible, you can't see it."

I paused, trying not to look panicked, but instead, to look spiritual.

"What about this verse on circumcision?" someone else asked. Ah ha! A way out. "It says here in chapter two, verse eleven that we are circumcised with a spiritual circumcision."

"Good question. What do you make of it?" I asked him. He was a war veteran, a longtime government employee, who now in old age would watch the demons play on his car outside his house. They were friendly demons. And he knew they weren't real. But he still saw them. He never spoke up in class, so this was a chance to encourage him.

"What if you don't have to get circumcised?"

"Well, we don't, as Christians—we think of the removal of evil from our hearts, rather than of flesh from the body."

He stared. This isn't what he meant.

"What if the thing they cut off wasn't there from the beginning?"

"The foreskin?"

"Yeah." Were we really having this conversation in Sunday school?

"Well, then, I guess you have a leg up on us in understanding this." A leg up. Nice. I should've just asked for more information about his private parts.

They looked at me. Isn't it a marvel they come back to Sunday school, with answers this unhelpful?

The older adults' class (average age, seventy) actually ordered curricula (likely the doing of one of the retired ministers in there). Like Lester, and like the teachers of the older adults' class (youngest participant, sixty), I ignored that curricula when they asked me to teach. I'd do, well, pretty much what Lester did: wait for the Spirit to strike (not always in front of my TV, but sometimes), run that topic through a concordance, and show up with what I had to teach. Just because Lester's class ran back to the Spirit and America and mine to Jesus and the church doesn't make mine any less subjective.

It was hard to get the conversation in the older adults' class to go any farther than a random pronouncement by someone or other. Once I asked them, "Why do we come to church to worship God?"

Ted, who hadn't been to church in a while, didn't seem to think one had to. "I'd just as soon talk to God in my yard."

"Why?"

"Well, if I see a stick, I can go and pick it up. Throw it away if I want to."

We looked at each other.

"OK, next question. . . ."

Ted's uncle beat an incumbent state legislator, Jim, who went to Jaylynn's church. I asked Ted about it once. "Mama said her brother would never beat Jim," he said. I asked Jim about it later. "Really? His mama said that?" He left unasked the obvious question: then why'd he run—and beat me?! Small-town politics is . . . small.

Back at my church, Candidate Landis, Dan Landis that is, was a longtime teacher of the older adults' class. His nemesis, the upstart running against him, was Lester. Lester Clinton. Even though Lester was older and Dan was younger, Lester taught the younger adults and Dan the older adults. Don't ask for the logic.

After his election loss, Dan taught his normal Sunday school class. He had warned me he was going to close with a request for a break from teaching— a move as unprecedented as a Third-World dictator quietly retiring. As he launched in he got emotional. "People aren't always what they say they are," he said, cryptically. "We're going to look around at some other churches," he said, voice breaking. He left without staying for small talk. Grown men don't cry in public in Zebulon County, and he wasn't about to if he could help it.

His longtime friend Jimmy, who was also close to Lester and the other campaign, hollered after him in the parking lot, "Dan, we don't want you to leave this church!" Dan said nothing, just waved, tried not to break.

And that's Sunday school at its best. The topic didn't matter so much. Whatever it was, occasionally, real life would break through, and grown men would indicate a need for one another's presence in the pew Sunday by Sunday.

Is it any surprise Dan came back?

Sneaking Sacraments Back In

My best effort to rectify the sagging content of these adult education meetings was to have weeknight Bible studies. Of course the old ladies came. Not because they came to everything (truth be told, they didn't). But they wanted to be supportive of me, and if it had "Bible" in it, they were game. So I hosted a "Bible study" on Rowan Williams's Lenten book for that year. He had been archbishop of Wales in the Church of England when he wrote it, but was now archbishop of Canterbury. And he was my favorite theologian: brilliant, but not showy; wise and good, but not at all sweet, like Gandalf—I would follow him around like a Hobbit if I could. He even talked about the Bible a little.

Ellen was willing to come to support me, but she wasn't at all sure about Rowan.

"Is he one of us?" she asked.

"Well, he's not Methodist, but he's archbishop of Canterbury."

She blinked at me. I might as well as said he was the Zerglon of Morff for how helpful that was.

"But is he a Christian?" she asked.

This gap in our communication was indicative of those studies. In another instance I invited a group to go see Mel Gibson's *Passion of the Christ* together. It was an important movie in our wider culture, they were hearing about it, we academia types were talking about it at Duke, surely it made sense to go. Plus moviegoing was a way to appeal to a younger group, to be hip and with it, to do theology in a post-textual world.

The youngest attender was age seventy-five. Amy, bless her heart, sat beside me in the theater. Over the din of the previews she whispered to me, "I haven't been in a movie theater in twenty-five years." At least, with the thunderous sound level, she had no problem hearing. I asked her why she had come. "We wanted to support you," she said. At least I think that's what she said, over the surround sound.

Afterward I regaled them on the dangers of anti-Semitism in Mel's movie, which we should be especially keen to avoid in a time when that cancer is on the rise in Europe and elsewhere. Roscoe looked at me gently. He had no idea what I was talking about. But he was glad I seemed to be happy up there, lecturing them as their teacher. "It was a little too violent for me," was all he said.

In sharp contrast to these failed adult ed approaches, we had the best success with special worship services on holy days. And these on holy days they hardly knew existed. March 25—Annunciation Day—precisely nine months before Jesus' birth. The Martyrology of Jerome pronounces that "on March 25, our Lord Jesus Christ was crucified, conceived, and the world was made."[1] It is perfectly fitting, the ancient church thought, that Jesus should die on the day he was conceived—a symmetrical life cycle. Further, and this is the blindingly beautiful part—the world should have been created that day. For creation has to be understood through the re-creation that is salvation; or, said differently, Christ's resurrection is the eighth day of creation. It is the same God who creates and who saves; and salvation has to do with the reclamation by that God of all that is material. It's a gorgeous vision.

So we would gather for worship that evening, as we would also for All Saints' Day or Ascension Day (I gave them a few old favorites too, like Thanksgiving). And those services would be . . . different. No choir. No offering. No announcements (thank God). No bulletins. No special decoration. Just God's people, God's house, in worship, listening to preaching, partaking of sacrament, with it all bookended by joyous greeting and parting. Somehow the physical act of leaving the television for the evening and venturing out to church for some odd occasion, one that would have to be justified to self and spouse ("You see, Ascension is the day when . . ."), punctuated with unfamiliar hymns and a new theme of preaching, in the same house with the same sacraments—it all *worked*. It made preachin' (as they, and I for those years, defined my job) worth doing. In only a few minutes, with no warm-up jokes or overwrought illustrations, I would explain the feast day and what it meant for our lives. They never lost interest. It felt like the eternal *now* that heaven is, with the presence of Jesus and all the saints, all filtered through the prism of one liturgical event. Perhaps even the angels bowed.

For Maundy Thursday service we would wash feet. They'd never done this before. They came forward a bit haltingly in church, unshod in that place for the first time, faces beaming like kids getting away with something. I'd wash, they'd smile, some would hug me.

---

1. See here Gary Anderson's *The Genesis of Perfection: Adam and Eve in Jewish and Christian Imagination* (Louisville: Westminster, 2001).

Then *she* came. Our hardest-working member. Up at 5:00 to make biscuits at Hardee's. Supporting more family members than I can count, maybe than she can.

And did those feet ever show it. Gnarled, bloodied, blue, misshapen. "I told Granny not to come, you wouldn't like her nasty old feet," her great-grand-daughter told me. In a worldly sense, no, indeed not. In a ministerial one? It was like washing Jesus' own. They were precious, more than if they'd been shod in satin and pedicured. It was a moment that makes a job like this worth doing.

"Next year I should wash yours," she said.

CHAPTER NINETEEN

God's Patience
and Ours

Methodist ministers are meant to be one another's church. Once we're ordained or serving a church (these are two different things for us, weirdly), we belong to a local church no longer. We belong to the annual conference, which meets once a year and otherwise "exists" as a sort of virtual church and a conglomerate of smaller meetings. So when we marry or change jobs or retire or die it's the annual conference that announces this in its journals, celebrates or mourns at its meetings, and not the local congregation. It is odd to devote oneself to life in the church and then immediately be removed from it, but that's the way it is.

Theoretically then other ministers should be our fellow church members. This was no small thing to John Wesley. He organized the early Methodists into holy clubs—small groups that would sit down together, read Scripture, pray, and inquire into one another's lives. "So, who sinned this week?" a leader would ask, and others would respond. Megachurches have mastered this aspect of the small group that we've forgotten, ironically enough—Willow Creek would not be as big as it is had it not insisted upon getting people into small groups. They can be organized by neighborhood, interests, likes or dislikes, it almost doesn't matter—you have to have someone eating in someone else's living room or they won't come back. If you get them there they will—by the tens of thousands. Willow is the Methodist movement writ large. And it was always thus. Tom Albin has shown that most early Methodist conversions came through small groups, not through outdoor preaching. Small groups being the way to church growth, it makes sense to organize preachers into a group to provide spiritual nurture to one another.[1]

---

1. See his "An Empirical Study of Early Methodist Spirituality," in *Wesleyan Theology Today: A Bicentennial Consultation*, ed. Theodore Runyon (Nashville: Kingswood, 1985).

So how come other Methodist ministers are such a pain in the ass?

Jaylynn and I would attend district meetings of clergy—required gatherings dressed up to be jolly but generally pretty torturous—and be met there with only cold stares. We were on our own to interpret silence. Are these ministers afraid we might move in on their turf? Do new ministers of these part-time or multipoint charges come and go so often there's no point even learning their names? Or do they just not give a damn? With this sort of treatment in our (mobile) workplace, we can see why skewerings of office culture like *The Office, Office Space,* and *Dilbert* have such an audience. And they're not even playing the God card.

We liked one local pastor, Bert, well enough, admired his work at his church. One Sunday Jaylynn got an infusion of visitors. She was thrilled. Maybe word had gotten out about her preaching, her pastoral care, her ministry generally? No such luck. Bert had hired a black organist. His racist refugees were looking for haven. Jaylynn sent them back to Bert. We immediately liked him more. Did he want to get together for dinner, perhaps with his wife and all our kids?

"Sure!" he emoted. "Any time! When? Well, we're busy this week. And next. And next." Last time we asked him he said, "After conference." It never happened.

Often we younger ministers band together. We're in cahoots because we're going to change things, make them better, make the church more tolerant and reach the world for Christ all at the same time. But then at other times we're in one another's way. A successor at one of our churches paused when we asked how things were going. "Not good, I'm leaving," he said. "Really? What went wrong?" "Well, they weren't really ready for my coming. Finances were in disarray, people's leadership was ill defined, it's sort of like they were rudderless when I got here."

Was he really saying this about *our* ministry as his predecessor? We tried to stick up for ourselves. "Well, yeah, like we told you, this wouldn't be easy but the people are sweet, and the house is great to live in."

"Uh huh. Except for the mice and the snakes."

No love from our fellow Gen X'er even.

There is something about the itinerant system in Methodism that makes us worse competitors with one another than ministers in other systems. Presbyterians and Episcopalians and Baptists and other sorts of polities get to hire their people. So they may eventually "compete" with a friend at the next church over for a job elsewhere, but it's unlikely, since the field of possible destinations is national. The pool is so much larger their next church could well be states away. But we Methodists know there are only so many spots to move up to, and more people who want 'em than can have 'em. Even we who were on the bottom of the food chain seemed to evoke fear in those somewhat above. Or at least unfriendliness. We might move up ahead of them. Take their pay raise. Do really well in our church and make them look bad in theirs. Something, anything, that would challenge their fat asses to get off the couch, out into the community ministering, into the library thinking, into the church praying, instead of on the golf course or in front of the TV.

Maybe I shouldn't be surprised they felt threatened.

We've been around a fair number of retired ministers in our five different local churches. It seemed to me as an active young minister that being a retired minister should be the easiest thing in the world. It's like being a grandparent or pastor's spouse, only with even less responsibility. Smile ceaselessly. Laugh at all the jokes. Nod at all the sermon's profound points. Indicate support in meetings. In short, be the model parishioner you wish all your own had been for you. It really can't be hard, can it?

But one of our retired ministers found this a tad difficult. It's not that he'd had an illustrious ministerial career himself there in exurban Illinois—he pastored a few churches, dropped out and got a proper job, teaching at the local high school. He did a great deal of good there, no doubt. Won some teaching awards. But he still spoke and acted as though he were once the darling of the seminary, the apple of his professor's eye, the brightest student in the class, and the "one that got away" for the connection of Methodist preachers. And he had no problem invoking this faux legacy in public against me.

"What do you think of this phrase, 'In the beginning was the Word'?" I asked.

This is how I teach Sunday school—trying to draw out their thoughts and not just drop my own on their heads. I figure I can sneak in my stuff better, and they'll hear me, if I've really heard them first. The church's older people didn't always like it. Even I didn't always like it. You got what people thought. That's both its strength and its bane. But one consideration trumps: if they're asked to participate they'll stay awake. You'll hear what they think (well, what the ones willing to talk think, anyway). And, once in a while, you'll be surprised. More than once I heard something more brilliant than any commentary I'd read on the subject. "When I hear about someone's word, I think of their bond, their promise they'll be there," someone said. "If you break that you're nothing. God don't break that." Brilliant. It's spot-on. And without the years of biblical training, Greek, and all the rest. "Wow, that's great," I stammered.

"Hold on a minute, what about the influence of Greek thought here?" This interruption brought to you by the insecure retired pastor, John. "That way of thinking was simply foreign to the Hebrews. Greek thought was timeless, abstract, perfect for the Johannine community." They all looked at one another. He was in the back where they couldn't see him without contorting around in the pew. To their eternal credit they didn't roll their eyes, as I would have, as I am now.

This is the great secret of the small, local church. It is God's greatest cultivator of patience. It has to be or the roof will blow off. People can say bizarre, outlandish things in there, and others will still show up on Sundays. More, they'll bring them covered dishes (Zebulon's version of casseroles) when their spouses die. They're well aware of who's smart, who's off a little in the head, who's just precious, and what everyone else thinks. They've heard one another's stories a thousand times. And they'll sit there and let one another tell them again. They'd heard this from John before. And they still had no idea what the devil he was talking about.

I knew. He was giving the up-to-the-minute state of scholarship circa 1963. Back when he'd been that prized pupil in seminary he'd been taught this Hebrew/Hellenic distinction. It is now being questioned by many scholars in the academy, and is usually only brought up to be refuted. It's still out there in the water—once an idea is challenged it takes years for seminarians trained in it to die off and quit distributing it to laypeople, like so many sleep-aid pills. John hadn't gotten the memo and was regaling the Sunday school group with notions of Hellenic thought. And who the hell cared?

I was up at the podium, pen in hand, trying to act like I might write this buffoonery down. I couldn't dress him down for not reading the assignment, as I could have as a TA back at Duke (having grading power has its advantages). Nor could I be any less respectful than his parishioners in the room. They'd borne with him for decades. I, for a few months. I asked one of them later about John. "Aw, he just likes to talk," he said, with the patience the saints reserve for preachers and professors.

Of course the latest, most brilliant idea I deigned to drop into their minds in 2002 would one day not too far off be as dated as John's scholarship. Decades hence some other smarty pants from the local university would come and question my questioning of the Hellenic thesis, with good evidence from primary and secondary sources to back it up. If there is any justice I'll be the retired minister at that point—convinced my role is to keep the kid from falling off the rails, with the new things they teach the kids these days. I'll fume, especially if I remembered promise in a career that hadn't panned out. But hopefully he or she will learn a more important lesson about tolerance. Or, better said, patience—a biblical, theological virtue that takes years to master. Decades even. The small local church is a place to learn it. Most don't bother now.

God's patience is the time and space we live in at this stage of world history. This time between Jesus' ascension and his return is a grand time of God's patience— God's waiting for persons and societies to turn to his grace, or else to go our own way. Most of us do the latter. And how God bears with it we can never know. Whatever other virtues our Lord distributes to us through his church—love, joy, peace, and all the rest—why is patience so hard to pick up, when it's so central to God's heart and present way with the world? Whatever outrages we commit against one another, God bears them as patiently as he bore the crucifixion of his Son at our hands. And we're unwilling to be patient with one another in Sunday school?

It took a retired minister, rather than a new one, to teach me patience. He came calling after I'd been at Zebulon a while. Gene had been a minister of the United Church of Christ at big churches in New England. He spoke with a Yankee accent as pronounced as our Southern drawl. Discussing whether to baptize people who aren't members he gazed at me intently, "Are yu shore yu waaant to hold baack the graace of Guawd?" I sure didn't, especially after hearing that from him. I mean, he was wrong of course—refusing to baptize isn't withholding God's grace, it's being disciplined about who's genuinely a church member and who's not. But he was a saint. You listen to saints.

Gene had pastored big churches, gone to Union Theological Seminary in New York during its glory days, read publications like the *Harvard Divinity Bulletin*. His wife had classical training as a musician. When she played the hymns she actually read the music—she didn't just have the tunes memorized. They brought their sons with them from New England and bought a horse farm on more land than any minister could've imagined being able to afford in Boston since the pilgrims. They came out to church for every event we had, learning their way around covered dishes, with the collard greens and fried fried fried chicken that their lean frames suggested they didn't really eat if they could help it. Leslie even sang a benefit concert for a fund-raiser for us. They weren't Zebulon County, they were "from off" as some country people around here say. But they became part of it. When I told them I was leaving I was sure they'd be leaving too. Surely their only connection to this little bitty church in the country was a fellow civilized person with a divinity degree who could discuss Richard Niebuhr. "Oh no," Gene said, "this is our 'chuch' now." No Rs.

"That was really great," Gene would say after a sermon. "I'd never thought of that." Well of course he had, if it was any good he'd already preached it, if not . . .

Maybe we got on so well because he wasn't Methodist. I'm told that many clergy find their best friend in town among clergy from another denomination. There's no possibility of competition, and yet you understand the same stuff, likely hold the same politics, and you probably both ain't from 'round here. Gene certainly wasn't from around here, and my being from an hour away made me no less an outsider.

But here again the local church's patience astounds. We ministers are a pain in general, not least the young'uns. Just think—as soon as I was gone, another smart aleck kid from Duke would come that way to try her or his wiles on them on the way to moving up to another, fancier job somewhere that matters more. And the local church takes it. Even celebrates it. They train pastors and other people in other churches reap the benefits. It's their role in the body, they accept it, and don't complain about it. We preachers are unworthy of such laypeople.

"Either you follow a turkey, you are followed by a turkey, or you are a turkey," one minister friend told me, and among Methodists he might be right. But you'd never know it from talking to Beech Grovers. "We were blessed with Paul, blessed with you, and now we're blessed with the new preacher," one told me recently. I could have rebuffed her by recounting our very different gifts. Paul was a retired Navy chaplain. My successor is now an associate at a fancy church on the ministerial fast track to greatness. Maybe she just meant we were all competent, showed up when we were supposed to, did our job, didn't steal or sleep with anybody we shouldn't. Or maybe she's figured out that the way to grow in this church is to love the minister, sent by God as she or he is, and receive what they say and do as a gift—a strange one sometimes—but a gift nonetheless.

CHAPTER TWENTY

Be of the Same Mind
in the Lord[1]

I had a case of Euodia and Syntyche at my church. Only it didn't turn out as well as Paul's did.

Or did it? We assume that because of Paul's soaring rhetoric in Philippians, his unassailable biblical logic about the incarnation and human community, that these two leaders at Philippi reconciled. But the Bible doesn't tell us that. Paul makes an appeal to them at 4:2 to be reconciled and . . . what? In a similar case there is an Eastern Orthodox iconographic depiction I love of the reconciliation of Peter and Paul. The two apostles embrace, moving as dynamically as anyone ever does in the molasses medium of iconography, gold background signifying the truth of this hagiography.

Where's that happen in the Bible, you ask?

It doesn't.

Peter and Paul had a row of some sort, as Paul triumphantly relates in Galatians 2. The history of the church attests that Paul's side won out and kosher laws ought not keep Jewish and Gentile Christians from eating together. Eastern Orthodox Christians take these data and assume their correlate: Peter and Paul later reconciled. How could they not? The gospel makes friends out of enemies, after all. Two of the pillars of the building couldn't be permanently pulled apart or the whole would have collapsed. So there they are in gold, embracing, all based on an assumption that can't be proved.

My Euodia and Syntyche are both wonderful women—vivacious, funny, dedicated to their church, in love with their families. They just couldn't get along with each other. One, Tracy, volunteered tirelessly at church, as was only fitting

---

1. See Philippians 2:2.

for an adult member in the congregation where she was baptized and brought up in faith. Her parents and grandparents and great-grandparents attended and people still talked about how wonderful they all were. She was the church's darling, its baby, one of the few who had stayed. She went up to Danville to work and meet her husband and live, but still worshiped back home in Zebulon, surely winning the prize for longest drive on Sunday mornings and Wednesday nights and whenever else the door was open. She'd tried to nudge her fellow church members toward more contemporary forms of church music, and has succeeded where many other churches have dashed themselves against the rocks. The result is not always pretty—soloists whose spirits are willing but flesh weak belt out contemporary tunes to canned CD music—but it is Beech Grove's effort to keep with the times. I often wondered if we went so willingly because of Tracy's gracious spirit about the thing.

The other, Rachel, was more clearly an outsider to the community. But she'd been there for years. That's the way it is, even in a quite-welcoming rural church like mine—everybody knows if you're new or if you're old time, and the latter comes when you can point to grandparents buried in the church yard. Rachel had baptized one of her daughters there, too, after marrying locally and they all lived right down the street. She and her husband kept goats that managed occasionally to wile their way outside the fence and down the street and over a few blocks to the church. Two trustees went to mow one Saturday and were attacked by a vicious creature with horns and hooves (no pitchfork though). One was knocked over before the other shooed him away and called somebody with a truck and some know-how. Good thing we paid the insurance premiums that month. I could see why Jesus chose these creatures for the critters on his left hand in Matthew 25.

Rachel had a toughness I admired from the beginning. When I asked her her name for the third time she made a not-unkind face that said, "I'm about to get impatient with you, Mr. New Preacher, but not yet." She brought family to church when they were in town, and once a month in the summer led the children's group, who went to do something fun around town, insofar as they could find such a thing. She laughed at my jokes and nodded vigorously when I preached once about salvation being like adoption. "We tend to think of adoption as a consolation prize to natural birth," I said, "but for Paul in Romans salvation is more like adoption than anything else. So what's 'normal'?" A preacher flailing around will always remember who throws them a lifeline, and Rachel did.

She loved her two daughters, as all mothers do, but perhaps with a touch more of the toughness that was part of her character. I don't know why, but one wonders. Was it hard to get pregnant? Had they considered adopting more kids than their two? Whatever combination of personality and circumstance led to a shielding of her children that is not unsurprising in mothers. As a child of a mother who was often a mess and unable to help me, let alone protect me, I saw something fiercely maternal in Rachel, and I loved it.

Rachel's place was big enough to have been a farm once, even if they weren't farming now. They loved animals. Rachel opened a little antique shop on their property. Parishioners remembered when Ms. So-and-So had run a store in that same spot, back when it was a dirt road and a car could pull right up, let a kid out, who'd go in and buy candy for impossibly small sums of money. "We're reopening!" she announced, to friendly smiles, but little enthusiasm. The store had little bits of antique junk, some sweets, and Rachel. I can't imagine it ever sold a thing. But it was gorgeous, in a creaky-floor-rusty-treasure sort of way, and I liked stopping in to chat with her about the old deck of playing cards she'd found or the cookies she'd made. It was downhome and largely customer-free.

Rachel's husband, Tripp, had once been a local sports star before blowing out a shoulder. He had designs on being a local politician, along with his work in the real estate business. He could do it—he was active, smart, opinionated, and got along with everyone. But he was young and misjudged when to run, getting trounced in his first election for the state house. When I saw him after the election and consoled him he remembered previous disappointments—losing that shoulder when he could've made it as a ballplayer, among others. I didn't recognize the sound that came next until I looked at him, sobbing. "I see the kids getting off the bus and I know I could help their schools from our district," he said. I consoled him, praying that he and Rachel would hear God's yes to their prayer for gaining political office, even if it was appended to a more dread word, *later*.

I never had this sort of intimate pastoral experience with Tracy, the darling baby of Beech Grove. Maybe I would have if I'd stayed longer, seen her through a crisis of some sort, but maybe not—others simply don't need this sort of presence from their pastor. It is a holy, frightening thing to be invited into another's life like this. It'd be an obscenity to be present amidst death, new life, disappointment, thrills of joy, if one weren't there as a representative of Christ and his church—unless we're wearing Christ's robes, standing there as his representative, we're mere voyeurs. Being in that place leaves a bond that, once broken, doesn't go away. It just dangles.

I loved both Rachel and Tracy. I just couldn't figure out how to get them to love each other.

Rachel brought her eldest daughter late to practice for a cantata that Tracy had organized. She'd also missed some previous practices. God knows why. She was active, involved with sports, or was traveling, who knows. But she hadn't been there, and Tracy was hot. "Samantha has just come to be part of our show," she announced to the other children, "and we don't have a part for her. Is someone willing to give up their part?" No one was. Rachel, standing there, felt humiliated. How dare she draw attention to Sam's not having been here, and make someone else give up their part for her! Tracy, trying to be professional, was annoyed at Rachel's cavalier treatment of the program she'd been planning for months and rehearsing for weeks. Rachel felt singled out, called a bad Christian for not having had her daughter there, and mistreated for the last time as an out-sider. She told Tracy as much. I wasn't there, but word got to me quickly. It does that when people have words publicly.

Rachel wanted me to call Tracy in and tell her she was wrong, in no uncertain terms. "These people always treat me this way!" she said, remembering her out-sider status despite years of faithful attendance and service. "It can't go on like this! We're *leaving* unless she apologizes."

I was ready for this. I had Euodia and Syntyche in mind as I went to Tracy and asked her to sit down with me and Rachel. Not to make her apologize—I was quite sure both parties were in the wrong. But to talk things out. Make space for mutual forgiveness to help relationships go forward. If both would put aside long-term personal grievances, the whole church could be helped, not only because Rachel would stay but also because we'd be building a culture of reconciliation.

Tracy didn't want to come. I asked her to anyway, and she agreed. "I don't think it'll do any good," she warned me. I chalked up a minor ministry victory—having gotten both parties to agree to talk—and called it a day.

Planning this parley was the right idea in the abstract. Wounds unspoken sim-ply grow bitter, inciting biting comments, longer memories, deeper wounds, and finally a poisoned relationship. Better to get it all in the open. Address the pain, reconcile, do what Jesus wanted, all the rest of it.

But things didn't start well. "How dare you treat me that way," Rachel began. "I'm an outsider here and you never miss a chance to remind me." "You are not an outsider, you are loved here, and I wanted nothing more than to have Sam in the cantata." "You didn't act like it." "You didn't give me a chance to act like it." "You've never wanted a chance before." "That's not fair."

By the end Tracy slinked out. "I shouldn't have come," she said, not to me, not really to anyone, just saying the way it is. Indeed she shouldn't have. I'd learned something was the way it was in seminary, and used personal ties to push these women through the machine of my expectations for church. No wonder they came out mangled.

Tripp, Rachel's husband, quit coming to church meetings. He was pleasant as could be when I saw him. But their daughter Sam would glare at me. Increasingly I saw them at the video store or the grocery store and not at church. Finally I went to see them. Rachel was even madder at me for making her talk to Tracy than Tracy had been. "Are you coming back?" I asked them. "No, how can we?" I took a breath. "OK, we need to have you give up your leadership positions then."

"What?!"

"Tripp's on committees where we need him, we can't simply leave him on there if you've decided to leave the church."

"How dare you."

She stormed out of their living room. Sam glared. Tripp changed the subject back to sports or politics. This was why he'd do well as a salesman or politician—

he could be pleasantest when no one else was. When I'd see them around town, Sam would look at me the way a Republican does a tax hike. Her face was a better indicator of the way the family talked about me than Tripp's friendliness. How would she grow up thinking about the church? Not just Beech Grove, but the church generally? What was it Jesus said about those who cause a little one to stumble?

I may have been right theologically, abstractly, enough to ace a quiz. Leadership positions aren't résumé builders or ego satisfiers. They actually have expectations that need to be met. An empty chair means more work for everybody else. If Tripp wasn't coming we needed someone else there. But it couldn't have done much to reassure Rachel in her sense of being a neglected outsider. And life isn't a quiz.

I asked recently when I visited whether Rachel and Tripp ever came around. They don't, I was told. There they are, just down the street, coming to nothing. When they pull out of their drive and head to school or the store, they must see the church sign and remember a place where they perceived less-than-full welcome, a minister they originally liked, but who turned out to bring out the worst of the church's exclusive ways. Will they ever pull out of that drive to go on to another church? I hope so, but I doubt it.

The mainline has struggled for decades now of decline. Interest groups in the church ascribe it either to leaving behind biblical truth or to failing to be open to the modern world. It's striking how far either of those claims are from Tracy or Rachel. The Bible *is* involved—I tried to get them to reconcile as Paul says we should. The modern world is too—a church can't be as hereditary a club as it once was and survive. Even Beech Grove was not entirely a family chapel anymore. Yet it was enough so to make people who'd been there for years feel like they didn't belong.

Isn't this how decline happens? A single pastoral failure at a time?

And maybe this is why large churches succeed. Tracy can avoid Rachel there, and vice versa. They can pay someone to direct stuff, attend another music program if there's friction with the first one, and run no risk of being dragged into the pastor's office for an exhausting free-for-all on who needs to apologize to whom. They might not even see their pastor, except on TV.

A friend rode in a cab once with a member of Willow Creek in Chicago. The cabbie praised Bill Hybels, pastor of Willow, even pulled out an autographed copy of a book by the great man, before dropping all his problems on my pastor friend's lap. My friend said, "I was present to him, gave him pastoral care, listened, hell I could even have prayed with him if I didn't feel weird about it. When's he getting that from Hybels?"

The small church is messy, it fails, it leaves no place to hide from one's enemies. And just so it's the sort of church Paul imagined. And who's to say Euodia and Syntyche reconciled? Maybe one slinked off or maybe they died at odds. Who knows? The Orthodox may be right, we may reconcile ultimately with a gold background and halos. But it might not be in this lifetime.

CHAPTER TWENTY-ONE

Deeper Wells of Peace

I t's because of Rachel and Tracy that I couldn't read Wendell Berry when I was a local church pastor. I tried. Everybody I knew who was smart read Berry. Everybody who was smart and who cared about rural churches seemed near about to memorize him. So I tried. And I got passages like this:

> One hot summer afternoon I saw Grover Gibbs passing along in front of Mr. Settle's garage with a plumber's helper over his shoulder. He saw, sticking out from beneath an automobile, Portly Jones's sweat-shiny big bald head, to the top of which, with a smooth and forceful underhanded thrust, he affixed the suction cup. . . . He allowed himself to be confronted by Portly, looking perhaps like a unicorn with a red face.[1]

Of course it's a funny image, man named Portly with a plunger on his bald head. But it seems to suggest a sort of sweetness to small-town life which isn't actually there. Maybe it never was. People were never any less cussedly violent and self-interested than they are now. Berry sounded to me like a kind of fantasy for 1950s wholesome American goodness. Ask any black friend whether she would have wanted to live in a small southern town in the 1950s. This was how I conceived of Berry.

With a little distance my view of him has matured. Berry writes fiction set in a place called Port William, loosely based on his own rural home on the Kentucky River. Maybe living in Port William itself, in my case in the form of

---

1. Wendell Berry, *Jayber Crow* (Berkeley: Counterpoint, 2005), 5.

Zebulon County, made it impossible to read about another Port William. Now, having been away, living among people who, like me, move for new jobs and better opportunities and so leave a transient wake of wreckage from previous cobbled-together lives, I can see the wisdom of Berry.

Some of it comes from his title character, Jayber, being a barber. He works in a shop where people come and dish gossip. They set a spell (it means "sit a while," not cast an incantation) even if they don't need to. And they talk. This is how "news" is disseminated before "The News" comes along via technologies like television, with its interplanetary talk of War and The Economy. The barber can see stories like the one of Portly and the plunger outside his window. My barber in Bartlett grew up in Gibsonville, North Carolina, with future NFL star Torry Holt. Said Holt wasn't such a bad guy. He even threw a big party for the whole town when he got drafted. He ain't forgot where he's from. That's news you can use, right there in the barber shop.

But there's a more basic activity to barbering than gossiping. It's cutting hair. I don't mean to be flip. There's something intimate about cutting hair. Handling someone's head. Just ask the guy in the *wrong* barber shop where I wandered into one day. The cobwebs should have warned me off. As soon as he said, "Oh, I didn't gap you, did I?" I knew how badly I'd erred, as the missing chunk from my sideburn made clear. A barber shop teaches you things, some of which you might not want to learn: "This was sometimes funny, as when I would get a suspicion of a kinship that was, you might say, unauthorized."[2] Jayber'd cut people's hair their whole lives, and their kids' and their grandkids' hair. And through so doing he came to understand what *membership* was.

> It was a community always disappointed in itself, disappointing its members, always trying to contain its divisions and make gentle its meanness, always failing and yet always preserving a sort of will toward goodwill. I knew that, in the midst of all the ignorance and error, this was a membership; it was the membership of Port William and of no other place on earth.[3]

He learned this through touching generations of heads of hair with gentleness and tenderness. Other people are trained to touch those same young men's heads with violence: "I cut the hair of Tom Coulter and Virgil Feltner and Jimmy Chatham and a good many more who went away to the various wars and never came back, or came back dead." Berry is deeply aware of the violence of small communities like Port William, like Zebulon County. The racism stinks. The small-mindedness. The pettiness. All the rest of it.

And yet. For all of that, there is in such places a well of peace that runs much deeper.

---

2. Ibid., 125.
3. Ibid., 205.

Somewhere underneath of all the politics, the ambition, the harsh talk, the violence, the will to destroy and waste and maim and burn, was this tenderness.
Tenderness born into madness, preservable only by suffering, and finally not
preservable at all. What can love do? Love waits, if it must, maybe forever . . .
Christ's wounds are still bleeding.[4]

It is that beauty, which I caught a glimpse of for just a moment, that is the
glory of small churches.

---

4. Ibid., 294-95.

CHAPTER TWENTY-TWO

Overdue Wisdom

I know why we Methodists have itinerancy. It is meant to keep things fresh, to keep ministers and congregations both from a kind of familiar ease with each other that dulls the sharp edge of the sword we wield weekly from the pulpit. I as a minister am supposed to find sufficient support (and job security) from itinerancy to say things to my congregation I wouldn't otherwise say. They, conversely, are comforted in the knowledge they will be spoken to prophetically, and that they will never become the sort of personality-cult church that other denominations sport. Most important to them, they will never have to waste time or energy on a search committee, and if they get hacked off enough, they can ask that the bishop move a preacher. As I remember my last two Sundays before moving, my last two chances to break bread and open Scripture with my church, when I wrestled with a new pastoral emotion: sadness. I saw the same on their faces. We had a terrific, all-too-short two years together, and we were sorry to see them end.

This sadness shed some new light for me on pastoral ministry. Had I known I would feel this way at the end, I may have begun things quite differently two years previous. For example, I am not sure that my sadness at the end did not conceal a certain pastoral pathology. That is, it may indicate an emotional dependence on my parish, rather than a priestly vocation to speak the truth in love. I deeply relished every "Good job, Preacher" that came my way Sundays at noon. I cherished every smile that greeted a pastoral visit, glad to have improved a lonely or hurting person's day, even just a little. I loved most of all the look of respect I received even when I just walked into a room.

When at church, I felt like I mattered. And perhaps just so, I failed as a minister. For that love of their company and respect may have kept me from saying things I ought to have said, about matters large and small. About how he talks too much, drowning out anyone else who might speak in Sunday school class.

About the dreadful theology, culled from the South's various fundamentalisms, that says America had better support Israel against the Palestinians or lose any blessing from God. About the one hundred pounds he ought to lose, lest he go on to glory land earlier than any of us wants. About the self-righteousness that poisons her long tenure as Sunday school teacher, no matter how grateful we are for her time and effort. About the "crisis" mode she is always in, almost *needing* some desperate prayer request to make it through each breathless day. About the racism that seeps from his jokes, stinking to high heaven, but not objected to by his preacher. Even the word of approval about the new car or fancy vacation, offered out of friendliness, could have been substituted for a prophetic warning about greed.

Of course, these words would have reduced the sadness at the end, and the happiness during my tenure there! They could have also built a reservoir of resentment and resulted in some painful comments back to me about the quality of my preaching and visitation and theology and motives. And just so, perhaps we would have gotten somewhere toward the truth-telling, mutual repentance, and reconciliation that ought to mark the kingdom of God.

Since the first day in seminary I heard that a minister must guard her or his boundaries. Don't let them have all of you or you'll be nibbled to death by ducks, I was told. Keep time to yourself, defend your family's space, take regular Sabbaths. Otherwise there will be nothing left to give them come time for church. I took this advice and kept my distance to some degree. Yet now I wonder. Could I not have thrown myself more deeply into the thick of their life together? What if I had participated in choir, as they asked me at the beginning? The music would have been no better, but perhaps that time with them would have offered opportunities for teaching, now lost forever. Perhaps the Sunday nights I guarded for myself could have been given away more liberally to the youth, who would have remembered the time gratefully. Could I have designed more midweek teaching opportunities? Sure, only the same five people would have come, but they would have been well served, and both I and they would have been stretched in salutary ways through the time together. How precisely does our pastoral re-emphasis on Sabbath and boundaries fit in with one who "emptied himself" completely in service to us? (Phil 2:7).

Another regret: I know no better now how to deal with the church's nationalism than I did when I arrived. The Fourth of July always seems to follow hard on the heels of a pastoral change. For my first one, the Scouts processed in with the flag, which everyone promptly pledged allegiance to. I did not, remembering all I had learned at Duke from Hauerwas and Willimon about the idolatry that passes for worship in American civil religion. They noticed, of course. One brave soul called to ask me about it. "I fear that pledging, in church, crosses the line from honoring one's country to worshiping it." She was confused, but respectful. "I disagree, and I hope no one will be mad or leave over it." No one was or did.

The next time around we did not pledge allegiance. Perhaps they remembered my silent protest the first time through. Yet we did have a soloist sing Lee Greenwood's "God Bless the U.S.A." and the procession of the flag remained. Not much of an improvement! Clearly they deferred to my unstated wishes to remove the pledge but had no understanding of why I felt how I did, let alone any ability to articulate a view of holy space that would not see it compromised by idolatrous symbols of the nation-state.

Perhaps a teaching opportunity was lost here. Immediately after the hurt following the first act of noncompliance on my part, I could have held a weeknight Bible study on church and state and articulated my position in full. They would not have liked what they heard, but they would have understood it more fully. Then they would have had another year of hearing me preach on all manner of issues—Israel and the nations, peace, love of enemies, greed, and pride and so forth—that would have filled in their initial unawareness of a Christianity that claims to supersede all other claims to lordship. Informed and angry would have been better than confused but respectfully distant.

Another lesson: in whatever parish I serve in the future, I will dedicate my first few weeks to knocking on the doors of people around the church and introducing myself, inviting them to come to worship. This seems so simple, so obvious, yet I never did it. I was too caught up in getting to know my parishioners and the church and its needs and figured those needs of outsiders could wait. I was too devoted to becoming their chaplain, rather than their minister. Yet there are so many unchurched and dechurched people right outside our doors, and they must feel we don't care whether they show up, for we so rarely, if ever, have gone to them. An initial dedication to this task would have also signaled to my church a desire to see us in outreach together, as a task at least as important as learning intricacies of the lives of those already in my parish.

One of the proudest accomplishments during our time together was the parsonage we built for my successor. It is a nicer house than I will live in for some time, perhaps ever. They have done the work, from fund-raising to building, and are right to feel proud. Yet I worry. We have done all this work to help ourselves, to guarantee our own future. What of those around us who are not United Methodist preachers who need housing? Can't we devote the considerable fundraising, organizing, and building skills we have shown in our parsonage project to housing the homeless, or those now inadequately housed? Or would such an effort exhaust the few people competent to do this sort of work? Would they have been emotionally and even physically unable to do it more than once? I don't know. But Scripture's call to bear one's cross may signal an answer.

I also realized by the end that some of the people I care about most in the world are members of this congregation. Yet that is not the same thing as to call them "friends." Friends are those for whom not just affection, but intimate personal knowledge is mutual. I know my parishioners fairly intimately—what they love, fear, hope for, work for, think is important. Yet they do not know me to that extent. To a degree I have remained a stranger among them. This is some-what understandable, given the great differences between post-farming rural community and a kid who grew up in Chapel Hill and was then in, by my count, twenty-fourth grade. If I had this to do over again, would I try harder to extend myself in actual friendship to those in my congregation? To have them know me in my least ministerial moments, as well as on Sundays, behind the pulpit, be-robed, preaching away? I don't know the answer to this question. Perhaps the desire to be "friends" is dangerously close to the overly dependent emotional connection described above as keeping us from prophetic speech to one another. Yet it would have been less lonely, more honest.

Here's a final note on leaving Beech Grove. My church was beautiful. Each member has taught me something about churchmanship, whether how to be a better church person, or how not to! Each has painfully patent weaknesses, as well as glorious gifts. And each, and all of them together, is an icon of the living Christ, an image of the Lord of the church. Some Sundays I walked in behind the choir during the prelude and was met with a wave of feeling for these peo-ple, an overwhelming sense of love, of being precisely where I ought to be at pre-cisely the right moment doing precisely the right thing. It's a great gift to feel this at least once in one's life. Preachers are those gifted to feel it Sunday by Sunday. Whatever other faults I or they bring to that meeting, it is beautiful. And for that, glory be to God.

That glimpse of beauty raises the question of why one would ever leave. I've worried about it a great deal since. The short answer is that we needed more money. A second kid was on the way, Jaylynn was hoping to stay home, and the figures wouldn't balance. I started sending out semipanicked e-mails and one came back from *Christian Century*, for whom I'd written a little, that they had a job as an editor open. I applied and away we went. "I thought you said you were going to be an associate pastor at a big church in Texas," Joanna said to me. She was right, I had said that, I even meant it. But the *Century* paid more. I didn't tell her that. I didn't have to. Her own kids left for similar reasons.

Small churches like Beech Grove get used to having the lowest paid ministers available. This doesn't always mean they're the worst ministers. It just means they're starting out. For that very reason they might be the most energetic. But they, we, certainly make new-pastor mistakes. Foisting my politics on them. Trying to make laypeople kiss and make up when just letting them be would have been wiser. Needing to ratchet down the academicese a notch, or seven. I watched them as I made these mistakes. They could tell I made them. But they never lowered the hammer the way I deserved. "You young, you got ambition," Roscoe said to me when I asked for money to help build a parsonage. "When you get older, settle down, you'll see there's more to life." Yeah, but how's that help me build a house?

Wendell Berry writes of the perpetually young ministers who visit his fictitious (but deeply true to life) rural church in Port William, Kentucky. "They seemed to have come from some Never-Never Land where the professionally devout were forever young."[1] How must I have looked to my seventy-year-olds, me, at age twenty-six? The one who replaced me was twenty-one. I promised them the next person would be twelve.

Berry pours it on next though: "The preachers were always young students from the seminary who wore, you might say, the mantle of power but not the mantle of knowledge." Ouch. "They wouldn't stay long enough to know where they were, for one thing." Now that's not entirely fair. I knew Bartlett and environs. I knew they created Brightleaf tobacco. Actually a slave named Slade did. His descendants, or those of his white masters anyway, were in Jaylynn's Buelah Church. After tobacco they were trying to get into being a tech corridor, or a bedroom community. Neither was working. So they built a film studio. Made a movie there. It was awful. *Last Lives* it was called. You can't get it from the rental place anywhere except Zebulon County. It never did play on a big screen. Went straight to video. Even if it did play on a big screen, Bartlett's theater closed decades ago. See? I know the place. Berry writes truly, "All the world is a mosaic of little places invisible to the powers that be."[2]

"They wear the mantle of power but not of knowledge." That may not be fair in my case. I wore the mantle of knowledge—university training and all that. But perhaps I lacked the mantle of wisdom. Of knowing when to speak a truth, as I saw it, and when to guard it. How much of pastoral ministry comes down to that?

The church I served, however, did not lack wisdom. They knew I would be there a little while and gone very quickly. And they never complained about it. It's the way things are. In fact, they may see clearly their role in the Methodist system. They get all the new ministers. Some are good. Some are not. But they all pass through places like Beech Grove. The good ones will go on to be *somebody* in *someplace*. The wider church will benefit from a future tall-steeple pastor, bishop, professor, whatever. Beech Grove will benefit some too from those few years of energy. And then they'll go back to doing their best raising up the best from the next new pastor that comes down the pike from never-never land, like the rookie league club in a major league system. They do the work, some other church somewhere else gets the benefit of wisdom the kid lacked with them.

They sent me away with tears and gifts and money. They deserved better than my leaving so quickly. They deserved someone who would stay with them forever. Would that it were possible.

---

1. *Jayber Crow* (Berkeley: Counterpoint, 2000), 160.
2. Ibid., 139.

CHAPTER TWENTY-THREE

There Is Now No Longer Jew nor Greek

An obvious reason people assume small, rural, Southern communities are places of greater violence than peace is their history with racism. As deep as the wells of peace are in rural communities, aren't the wells of specifically racial violence deeper?

That'd been my assumption on moving there. "Watch out up there," a former professor told us. "The Klan was big in those places." That shook us up. So we asked the DS, gingerly enough, "Are these folks, uh, Klanners?" He reassured us: they're well educated, leading citizens, not at all Klan types. Clearly he'd dealt with this sort of denunciation of country people by self-satisfied morally superior university people before.

Early in our time there, a friend of the church came by to do some pro bono work (most work on pastors' houses in such places is done gratis. Even when such workers could really use the money.). The man had a black employee with him he called "Loco." We referred to Loco as his slave. He was constantly happy, would snap to on the boss's orders, and, well, submit to being called "Loco." Undoubtedly if you asked them, both men would recoil at the suggestion there was anything racist about this arrangement. But it had a certain awkward familiarity to it. Another time some church folks were asked how they liked their coffee. "Hot and black, just like I like my women," one said. Nice. We said nothing, except to laugh with each other after they left about how stunningly outrageous the whole thing was. How courageous.

I was equipped to think about race by the university, as you can see. I'd actually helped TA a course on the black church in America. Willie Jennings is a beloved former teacher, and I still return to his work when I think on these things. He taught us that race is artificial—it's a construct that doesn't actually exist. It's similar to how Augustine thinks of sin. Sin is a lack—like a hole in a shirt or an eye that should work but doesn't. The real thing is grace—sin is a tragic absence that doesn't make sense and shouldn't. Augustine doesn't mean no one sins—just look out the window. He's trying to understand what the thing is. So too with race. It's something that was made up and foisted on a people to justify another people's ownership of them. It's not a real category. All it is, is something made up, imposed, so one group of people can enslave and oppress another. But this construct has made for a terrible history.

Want proof? The one-drop rule is proof. In Southern history if a child was born with even a drop of "black" blood, that child was necessarily black, and in no way white. But why should that be? Isn't it arbitrary? (In addition to being racist?) Why shouldn't one drop of "white" blood make a child white? Because blackness taints; whiteness must be guarded. It's absurd, preposterous, and yet we've thought that way, and the resulting body count is not small. The other proof of the arbitrariness is the ability of some people to pass in both cultures. They are light skinned enough to function as a white person in some settings, but can switch and function in black culture as a member and not an outsider just as well.

How do we unthink racism? Well, by doing more than thinking. It's not a subject that can just be thought out of—it has to be lived out of. And the church is an answer to it. A community born through baptism in which there is now "no longer Jew nor Greek, slave nor free, male nor female, but all are one in Christ Jesus" (Gal 3:28, paraphrased). Evangelical language has long spoken like St. Paul: *all* have sinned and come short of the glory of God. *All* can be redeemed through Christ. And the black church has been a place marked by resistance to slavery, Jim Crow, and oppression. The resources to resist racism are already there. You just have to go search them out.

So imagine my pleasure when I noticed there was a black church right across the street from Beech Grove United Methodist. Beech Grove Baptist was our black doppelganger, right across the road. Perfect! We'll get together. Have Bible studies. Choir exchanges. Preaching swaps. I'd been taught right and now I was going to lead right.

But then something happened. And something else. I got busy. And the exchange never took place. Here I was TA'ing one thing at the university and leading another way at the church. Race just never seemed to come up. For me, that is. For others, for African Americans, it was doubtless never not "up."

Race runs deep in Zebulon. So deep you don't see it. Patterns of life are shaped long before we get there and we slip into them. We didn't have black neighbors. Or black parishioners. Or black friends. Relationships only happened over economic exchange, and even then people got called things like "Loco." There were other places where blacks lived, worshiped, worked. If it sounds like Jim Crow, well, it may as well be.

And I did very little about it. But isn't it a conceit of a white liberal university-educated pastor from somewhere else to pass judgment on a place like Zebulon for this?

Once I went to visit with Geena, one of my biggest supporters, the spouse of my most avid supporter. Visiting with them, and calling it "work" was almost unfair. They were friends really, people I enjoyed being with, I should've been clear it was time off.

I walked in, and Geena was already visiting, with an African American woman.

"Wow, all kinds of people here today, aren't there?" I said. I had meant that lots of people were visiting—Geena had had minor surgery of some sort. But before the words were even out of my mouth I was mortified. Why don't you just say "Look, a black person" and ask her to fetch you something from the kitchen? You dumbass cracker.

I was only an hour by car from the university, was there helping teach, had meant to take on race as a big issue, and my first chance to talk to a living, breathing black person and I say something stupid, and borderline (or more) racist.

At the university people would have reacted, rightly calling me on a statement like this. Geena, and her friend, did not. "Well hello, Pastor, let me introduce you to my friend. We taught together at school thirty years, now we're both retired, and we still get together and gossip like schoolgirls, don't we?" I looked in her friend's eyes and saw there not judgment, but grace. This was going to be *my* issue, my crusade, and all I offer is ham-fisted lameness. And all I receive back is grace. That's peace in a small rural community with a history of violent racism, sure enough. No conceit, just a friendship that cuts the other direction, with no academic crowing about "speaking the truth to power" involved.

At least this put race back on the agenda for me. I asked a child of one of my older saints about her memory of race in the church. She was a white liberal still, but not a white liberal churchgoer. She'd moved to Raleigh, was established in business, still had her bleeding heart, still called Beech Grove home, but didn't worship Jesus much anymore. Good for us; we'd made a Democrat, just not a Christian.

"I remember in the sixties when King marched in Danville," she said. There had been a small riot, with some people hurt, and photos splashed around the world of violence in Danville. "The trustees met and asked what they'd do if one of these Northern troublemakers come to church," she said. "Planned on how they'd block the door." She saw my look of surprise. "But downstairs in youth group we had a teacher who was subversive," she said. "Teaching us to invite black friends to church, to our homes, that's what we sang about: 'Red and yellow, black and white, they are precious in his sight.' The church taught me to be from Zebulon County and not be racist."

There it is. Trustees upstairs planning to block King and friends (as though anybody had designs on a little country church down the highway!). And in the basement the youth are being taught by other parishioners to be welcoming. Wells of violence, deeper wells of peace—right underneath the sanctuary.

I told her I wanted to do some exchanges with Beech Grove Baptist. At this point her octogenarian mother spoke up. Of course this woman's mother had been the sort of parishioner who would have taught the kids that racism was a sin, even back in the 1960s. "Go slow on that," she said. "You don't want to lose your job over something like that." Note: this was 2003.

So one Sunday after church I approached Beech Grove Baptist. I knew I'd be nervous, but man, I was terrified. Trembling. People were looking at me. Here I was not 100 yards from my church, across the road, and I was quaking. Why? I'm a pastor, for crying out loud. This is a church. They'll welcome me. Are black Sunday churchgoers always this dressed up? Why did I just wear a polo? Do I look as dumb as I feel?

"Can I help you?" an older man asked. People were milling around tidying up after worship, as they would be at any church anywhere in the minutes after noon on Sunday. But they had all noticed me. Some had stopped to look. They weren't hostile looks. But they weren't merely curious ones either.

"I'd like to meet the pastor," I said. The man led me to his office. Pastor, like the rest of his parishioners, was far better dressed than I, the white pastor from across the road. His cuff links sparkled. I never even wore a tie.

"Forgive my lack of energy today," he said, with extraordinary formality, in no hurry to finish his sentences. "I was in a car accident, and am a little shaken up." I told him I was sorry to hear that. He was about to eat lunch. On fine china. Someone else was cooking for him. His wife? A parishioner? Why was my pulse still racing?

I told him I wanted to get to know him and his church. Maybe to have some exchanges of some sort. Be what Christians were supposed to be—the baptized, for whom race is washed away. "That'd be fine," he said, giving me his card.

When I called a few weeks later I asked for the pastor. "He's not here any longer," I was told curtly. He'd been let go. No explanation was forthcoming.

And that was it. My big interracial initiative. Gone to seed as my initial contact left town with no explanation. I wondered what he'd done, or not done, to get run off. I never went back.

"Congratulations," a black friend from school said to me sarcastically. I'd told him I had walked across the street to start a conversation about race that had gone nowhere. "That took real courage," he said, courageous himself enough to mock my pretension.

Here's the thing though: it did. I was scared. The patterns of life in a place like Zebulon are such that you *do* notice when a black person is in your parishioner's living room; that the Beech Grove Baptists *did* notice when I came calling. Those have been patterns of violence historically—when blacks showed up where they shouldn't they could be in real physical danger. That's not so much true now. Yet the patterns persist. I've noted the mildly racist jokes that linger in the place. When a Beech Grover would come back from the beach with a tan, someone would ask if they shouldn't be at the church across the street. A teenager at the church asked me once, "If Adam and Eve was white, where'd we get all these black people from?" If only it was always so overt. One usually has to go out of one's way both to see these patterns of life, of conversation, and even more so to break them.

"I'm not so sure about that," Ellen said when I asked about pulpit exchanges. I knew what she was worried about—black preaching in a white church where we didn't know how to respond might feel so awkward it'd do more harm than good. Then she had an answer. "What about a joint Bible study?" she said. She was ready. So would the rest of the prayer group ladies be. I never did it. I left soon after.

Here's the thing about race in that community. It wasn't all important. Some things were more important. Like Jesus. One of our poorest families, well, our only *poor* family, was a great-grandmother raising her two great-grandchildren. She was sixty-eight. Do the math: this family had been having kids young for generations. She was white. They were . . . something else. By the one-drop rule they were black. With some Hispanic mixed in. Who knows what.

That church took those great-grandchildren in from the beginning of their lives onward. Doris, the great-grandmother, had become a member when her husband died suddenly. She'd been Methodist back in the day, and so she started calling Methodist churches in the phone book, looking for a place for a funeral. She was still paying off the funeral home, years later, for that funeral. The pastor and the building were hers free. And my predecessor, bless him, had visited, comforted her, invited her and the kids to join. She brought headaches with her—the kids were a handful of trouble. Trouble at church, at school, early pregnancies, could never sit still or pay attention.

But they weren't white. And no one ever said anything about it.

There were problems in our relationship with the granddaughters, no doubt. Some amount of noblesse oblige—we had a family in-house whom we could help with Christmas every year. But they came to everything we did: prayer meeting, Bible school, special services, the works. And they were a mixed-race family. We were not an all-white church. Our desire and ability to help one family, and not to reach down, but include them in our fellowship, overcame any lingering racism that would've been directed toward those kids. And no crusading minister had to tell them to do it. They just did. They were Christian first, before they were whatever else. And God bless them for it.

CHAPTER TWENTY-FOUR

Anointing

I remember a parishioner at church saying to me one summer, "I was in the kiddie pool, and I saw the heavens opened, and the hands of God reached down and touched me. What do you think of that?" Impressive. Now, what meds did you say you were on?

It is striking just how much mental illness there is in small, rural communities. Maybe there just is that much mental illness everywhere, but most people, most communities, have developed the ability to shield it from most eyes. One leader of one of our churches struck both me and Jaylynn as, well, a little resigned to a less-than-stellar job. He was competent, likable, smart, efficient, we asked him to run everything we could think of because he did well. But we couldn't figure out a polite way to ask why he wasn't CEO of something or other.

Somebody found a way to tell us once. "He's had hard times," she said. "Times when he was a little off." She needn't have said more. He was well connected in that church with multiple generations of family and friends. They could break his fall if he fell again. But it was no good going back into the corporate world someplace fancy. The church was the beneficiary of the business world's loss.

Another woman at one of our churches had once been a great leader there. Led outings with the youth, directed music, sang, you name it. Now when she came she was statuelike. She'd blink when you'd say her name, like she was trying to remember not just who you were, but who she was. Then her customary countenance would return and her face would catch up with her hand's greeting.

This one took longer to learn about because it was more recent, more painful. She'd been home some and decided her neighbor was a demon. This demon had managed to curse much of what they were drinking in their own home. Her husband ought not leave since those demons made things dangerous. But not to worry if he had to—she'd keep an eye on the receptacles, to make sure they weren't poisoned.

This was another case folks knew about but didn't dwell on. They loved her and wanted her there, whatever mind she was in. And maybe she'd improve. Maybe not. They'd seen it all before.

Another of our members directed her illness at one of us. She was disabled not only mentally but also physically, and needed extra time to get everywhere. The handicapped accessible ramps on our small churches really are a godsend, a sign of invitation and hospitality, all the more for being a financial and spatial burden on everyone else. Every time we opened the church doors she was there, trusty husband in tow, directing traffic, granting her access. Somehow early on I developed the habit not only of hugging her on Sunday but kissing her cheek. I don't normally do this, but somehow it seemed right with someone who got less physical affection than most of us. She'd kiss me back. I did this knowing that, as they say, she was a bit off.

Perhaps we'd underestimated how important church leadership was to someone with few other social outlets. There was some committee or other that she wanted onto. Since it had actual power we were eager to keep her off of it. It's one thing to let people bake pies when they're a little off, it's another to let them have a say in determining the whole church's future. She was not invited to join the committee. And she wasn't happy about it.

"I could sue you!" she said to Jaylynn. "You discriminated against me for my disability. You don't like crippled people. Well, I'll show you." She left Jaylynn in tears. "Don't worry honey," others told her. "She does that to everybody. Sunday she'll be like nothin' happened." Sure enough, Sunday came, she and I kissed, Jaylynn preached, and we went home.

I could go on here. There was the man with the temporary dementia who went around the hospital showing everyone his favorite parts (which they didn't want to see). The other who was sure there were monsters in her line of vision everywhere, even at church. Sometimes they verged on the more religious. A friend has a homeless parishioner who processes in and out with the choir and clergy each week. She does so, she says, because she is an archbishop. And sure enough, if Methodists had archbishops, they should get to process. Hard to argue.

They speak to me about the stories of the supernatural in the Bible. Or, more properly speaking, angels, demons, and "powers and principalities," in Paul's language (technically, to work "supernaturally" is to do something one's nature doesn't allow. Flying would be supernatural for a human without a machine, but perfectly natural for an angel.). Jesus spent a great deal of his time casting out demons, especially in stories that dot the Synoptic Gospels and our lectionaries, and so lend themselves to countless demythologizing sermons about anything other than the demonic. The longer I was a pastor and bumped into these sorts of illnesses, the more I longed for Jesus' power to cast them out. We have more medicines to work against them, and perhaps just so, we seem to have less spiritual authority.

They also speak of what's wrong with our medical system. I remember well the hysteria that followed when a parishioner of mine in rural North Carolina decided to stop taking his medicine. His friends wanted me to intervene. Some interpreted it as a death wish. Others a cry for help. You'd have thought he had elected to take poison or gone and joined a cult or written a check to Benny Hinn. So as a dutiful pastor I went to try and talk sense into him.

He was a big, burly, athletic man, descendant of hardscrabble farmers whose hobbies included chopping wood and shooting things. He grew quiet when I asked him about the medicine.

"Used to be I felt good all the time. Then I got older and they made me take all them pills. And now I feel terrible."

He paused, uncomfortable, aware others would interpret his choice as sheer insanity.

"And now I feel good again. So I reckon I'm going to stay off the pills for a while."

Recently, after I'd left the pastorate at Beech Grove, a member was dying of cancer. The old ladies' prayer group naturally made it their practice to pray for Mac regularly. When there looked to be no medical possibility for him to get well, the ladies prayed accordingly. "They say there's nothing that can save him now," Mamie said. She paused. "Unless the Lord works a miracle." That "unless" means everything. In a culture in which we expect our medical industry to rectify everything, Christians still proclaim that we are ashes, and to ashes we'll return. Death is an enemy for us, but not an ultimate enemy. By the same token, the possibility, even infinitesimal, that the Lord may heal signals to the medical-industrial complex that we do not trust them entirely. They are not the final arbiter of our life and death—for all their God-given and hard-earned skill. We neither expect them to heal everything, nor to be sure when it's someone's time.

Mac died not long after. They had his funeral at the church. He was buried surrounded by people with his same last name. His widow mourned not anonymously, but nearby to family and church members. It's not perfect by any means. But it's good.

I was struck after another death as I watched the casserole brigade (sorry, the covered dish one) roll into the deceased person's house. A woman from another family—one not particularly close to the family who'd suffered this loss—brought in two dinners' worth of food, wheeled around and said, "I'm so sorry for your loss." These two might never be friends in the world's sense, might never say more to each other in church than "peace of Christ," might squabble over the budget or election or whatever at some point. But when someone died the other was there with fattening food to make sure the other could grieve without having to cook or clean. The church made their lives larger. Human beings were designed to love one another this way. I ache for those who don't have it. And yet we're so reticent to tell the story of how the church makes us more human.

Short of earthly healing, what's significant about these stories is how well the church amalgamates these persons into her life. Everyone knows everyone else's issues. And they cover for them. As Abba Moses liked to say to the other desert fathers, when he covered over another's sins in the community he was acting like God. Or as Pope John XXIII liked to say about spiritual leadership, "Overlook much. Correct a little."

Needy people still flock to the church. Many of these needy people had burned-out family relationships and strained friendships. Several had jobs that made space for their various disabilities but most lacked social outlets. And where were they welcome anytime they came? In church. Where a pastor would listen, everyone was glad they came, noticed when they didn't, and loved them. Really.

It's easy to bash the church. Many have had painful experiences there, myself, Jaylynn, and all these people likely included. The church is easy to bash because the church is full of knuckleheads, that is, human beings. We're all hypocrites, the greatest saints among us chiefly so. Unfortunately God has no one other than sinners to work with. But somehow the church has realized this, in her unspoken wisdom. She's made space for the strangest among us, allowed us to be that way, worshiped alongside us, cared for our children, wept when we buried parents, and been our friend and neighbor. It's a greater gift than any of us has a right to expect. It's like grace—God's own mercy. And the trick is—there's no batch of perfect people someplace else to replace this batch of sinners. Sinners are all God has to work with to get his way in the world. And it's all we have too.

This doesn't happen so automatically in megachurches. In megachurches anyone can walk in and be anything they like. Nobody has to tolerate you because nobody has to tolerate anybody any more than one has to get on with the guy in the movie theater next to you. I can see the appeal of this—I've had stages in my life when I wanted no one in my business as I worshiped Jesus. But those were stages. Everywhere, the church makes a place for crazy people because the church is full of 'em. That is, all of us. But in the small church you have to shake their hands. Weekly.

What the church is, really, is a crazy mother. She bears us. Nurtures us. Raises us. Makes our life possible. Then when we hit adolescence she embarrasses us. We wish she would go away. But there she is, announcing to all the world how uncool we are, setting us up for future therapy. Then finally we hit adulthood and realize we're more like her than we meant to be. And if she's ever gone, we miss her like hell. The church wounds us, like every parent wounds, hopefully unwittingly, penitentially, but in ways no less real. She marks us forever. And without her we'd not be us.

CHAPTER TWENTY-FIVE

Holy, Holy, Holy Lord

On a recent trip back to Zebulon I found out what had really mattered in my short two years of ministry there. No one talked about my scintillating preaching. Few did about the new parsonage, though there have been two subsequent ministers to live in the thing since we built it. Not even about my dazzlingly beautiful kids—can you believe it?

They talked about my singing.

Now, let's be clear: I didn't sing in the choir, as I've already said, and certainly didn't do solos. I wasn't above singing a line in a sermon once in a while. Anything to keep 'em from dozing, plus I envy priests and rabbis who *have* to sing, no matter how awful they are, to make it *work*. God requires song. You do it now. End of story. We don't have that. So I tried to supply it.

But the singing they meant was during communion. We did the eucharistic responses in song. I'd heard this from my mentor, whose singing voice and mine are like comparing the Lakers and your local Y pickup team. Who cared? I'd sing and then they would. And they loved it.

Originally I just meant it to get their noses out of the hymnal. I can't stand how much reading out of the damn book we do. We're supposed to be worshiping God, consecrating the elements, preparing to approach our Lord in bread and wine, and we're reading bold print, rote, dead, without attentiveness, out of a book.

So if I'd sing "Holy, holy, holy Lord," and they could reply, they'd look up at me. And smile. If I was singing, they could try. "God of power and might." Even the visitors would be with me now. "Heaven and earth are full of your glory." This line was higher, I'd usually miss it. They'd smile bigger. "Hosanna in the highest." But look at what we're saying—we're echoing, even participating in, the heavenly chorus that sang at Jesus' birth. "Blessed is he who comes in the name of the Lord." They'd call out just like the crowds at the Triumphal entry— here comes Jesus! Blessed is he! "Hosanna, in the highest." Hold that last note.

Then we'd get it, in our best moments. Church is preparation for a greater life to come. It's choir practice. We get ready our song we'll sing eternally.

"Christ has died." Monotone, I could hit that. "Christ is risen," slight inflection on the "ri-," still had it. "Christ will come again." They were still with me. It's the most beautiful words we'll say all week. Why not sing them? Loud and in unison?

"You know what I miss about your time here? The sangin'." I heard that over and over again. Not for any skill of mine. Just a willingness to be a little foolish and lead them in worship. That's being a minister. It's worth doing with the whole of one's life. And thank God for places like Zebulon County to do it in.

CHAPTER TWENTY-SIX

Cynical of Cynicism

I won't be the first person you've heard say this: my generation, thirty-somethings, have commitment issues. We like to keep our options open. We don't like to be tied down to anything. Our parents, in record numbers, divorced—breaking their promises to one another and to us. Better not to make such promises, we inferred. This not only makes planning an evening out difficult (yeah, I'll call you, later, maybe), it makes an institution as crucial as marriage that much more difficult. When I kept dallying on asking Jaylynn to marry me, *she* called the marriage counselor. "I hear you have commitment issues," the shrink told me over the phone. "Uh, yeah." "Well, why don't you come Tuesday at 9:00?" Finally—someone was telling me what to do! We were married within the year.

The danger of a generation with commitment issues is that we're susceptible to someone telling us what to do in frightening ways. Chris Hedges, an incisive journalist and writer with a sharp sword for an eye, keeps predicting that fascism will come to the United States wearing the Christian cross (for many critics of Christianity, fascism has long since already come). This is overblown. But what if the economic collapse of 2008 continued, a terrorist attack happened at a 9/11 level, and a demagogue came along right then, promising to save us? Would those without strong commitments to community, family, church, social organizations and so on, be more susceptible to that sort of secular savior?

We don't even have to raise the alarm level that high. Belonging, joining, being part of something bigger than ourselves—that's what makes life worth living. The most health-giving thing you can do right now is to go join a social organization of some sort. Meet with people. Work on something together. We're wired as human beings to want something to give our lives for. It's why corporations, the army, the university, whoever, have such an easy time getting young professionals to live and die for them. The problem is we're meant to give our lives to God in the church. That's the only place fit to bear that sort of existential weight. Those who give their very souls to their job or university or whatever, instead of to the church, invest them with a weight they cannot sustain.

So what happens to a generation designed, as all people are, to give ourselves to something bigger than ourselves, when we are reluctant to give ourselves to anything much more demanding of commitment than a game console or a social network Web page? We shrivel up. Become hollow. Shadows of selves.

The gospel promises the "life that really is life" (1 Tim 6:19). I've glimpsed this life primarily in one place: the small, local church.

St. Paul would not be surprised. For him, the Holy Spirit is not an ethereal thing given only to superbelievers who then babble in strange languages and coerce their friends to do the same (no offense to Pentecostals, generally). The Holy Spirit is love. Or even Love, we should say, capitalized. "Hope does not disappoint us, because God's love has been poured into our hearts through the Holy Spirit who has been given to us" (Rom 5:5). *Poured!* Like a waterfall, like an ocean going over a cliff, spilling out, running over, filling our hearts with life. Paul is speaking in the first-person plural here. We know these things. Together. We wouldn't have known them separately. The Spirit does not only groan within us when we lack words to pray, though of course, she does that (see Rom 8:22-27). The Spirit also knits us together, in the local church, across local churches, and through believers across space and time, all the way back to Jesus. We groan amidst this present trouble. We rejoice in hope that it will all be worth it. And the Spirit testifies to us that it is.

One Ash Wednesday my wife approached as I was dispensing ashes to people's foreheads, intoning, "Remember you are dust, and to dust you will return." She walked up with our one-year-old. He saw me, his eyes lit up with delight. I did as I was meant to do, drawing an ash cross on his forehead. "Remember *you* are dust, and to dust you will return." Even he, of the smooth skin and flush cheeks and seemingly eternally glad countenance. He'll be dust as surely as those people out there in that graveyard.

What a gift to give him a small church—a place to grow amidst others who know his name, notice his faults (and even correct them occasionally), celebrate his successes, teach him Jesus, feed him to him in bread and wine, celebrate his marriage, mourn his losses, tend him when sick, baptize his kids, and promise to mourn his death one day and await his promised resurrection in hope. Now that's worth committing oneself to.

Isn't God amazing? Especially in his gift of the small church.

Afterword

In the first days at my first parish I was deeply impressed with Georges Bernanos's *Diary of a Country Priest*. Bernanos's small French congregation was like mine in rural Georgia, right down to the manure and the mire, the feuding farmers, the apathetic confirmands, and the petty squabbles among the parishioners.

Though his small membership church was mine, I was not Bernanos. When he ecstatically exclaimed, "My parish! The words cannot even be spoken without a kind of soaring love," I felt ill. Perhaps if one is from the south of France rather than the honest-to-God South, a pre-Vatican II traditional Catholic rather than a post-1970s decline United Methodist, one is able to feel "soaring love" for the small church. I couldn't.

I still can't. Jason Byassee is about the best younger Christian scholar-journalist we have today, certainly one of our most eloquent commentators on the church. He opens this wonderful book declaring that "the small church is just God's primary way of saving people." Well, I guess. And his last word to us, after his loving encomium to the delight of the diminutive is "Isn't God amazing? Especially in his gift of the small church." Byassee's experience of the small church sounds somewhat like Bernanos. But their experience of the small church has rarely been mine.

The cynic in me says that this is the sort of book written by an eloquent, though idealistic young man who, though he says he loves the small church, made sure that he didn't stay in the small church long. Much of Jason's delight in the small North Carolina congregation he served is the wonderment of the outsider. His is the touristlike thrill of being a visitor among the Zulus. My view of ministry in the small church is more that of George Herbert, rather than that of Bernanos or Byassee. In *The Country Parson* Herbert says "the two highest points of Life" for the country parson are "Patience" and an ability to endure "Mortification." Herbert and I served the same small church, he in seventeenth-century England, I in twentieth-century Georgia.

What Jason experienced as love, community, and charming homespun fidelity in his small church I have more often seen as deadly, clublike interiority, insufferable pettiness, and maddening small-spiritedness. In most of my ministry I have therefore agreed with a friend (who left the parish for a ministry selling bathroom cleaner with Amway after a losing bout with two small churches), "The best view of small church is through your rearview mirror as your car kicks up gravel on your way the hell out!"

My antipathy toward the small church that Byassee loves may be partly dismissed as the cynicism of a church bureaucrat who struggles daily with the stranglehold of the small church on my church family, the United Methodists. Don't accuse me of describing a church I know nothing about—we Methodists have more small-membership congregations than any other church in all of Christendom. We have so many small churches not because they are so faithful but rather because we have the world's most expensive program for the subsidy of small churches and because bishops like me can force a pastor to serve a small church. Small congregations in any other denomination wouldn't have a prayer of attracting a pastor the quality of Byassee. Only Methodist bishops can make a pastor do that.

The most threatened and feeble congregations in my denomination are not like the small church Byassee describes; it's our middle-sized congregations and our large urban congregations that are in a slide. Small congregations have proved themselves to be doggedly resilient. They are the fastest growing segment, in sheer numbers of congregations, in all of United Methodism. Though our seminary-trained preachers have become too expensive to serve them, and though most of our clergy avoid them like the plague, and though most of our new Christians come in through our larger congregations, there is no indication that the plethora of small churches will go away. When the denomination with all its creaking machinery has passed into oblivion, when bishops like me have faded into justly deserved obscurity, the good country folk that Byassee describes in this book will still be there next Sunday, praising God, duking it out with one another after potluck suppers, passing the faith on to their young, burying their dead, complaining about the District Superintendent, trying to put up with one another in the body of Christ, and will continue to be the face of most of mainline Protestant Christianity.

How to account for Jason's remarkably gentle, loving, generous eloquence toward the small church? His heartfelt gratitude for the small church is more than that of a younger pastor who one day shall be as decrepitly derisive as I. God has given Jason Byassee a gift for seeing the small church *sub specie aeternatis*. He has been given the gift of looking at the small-membership church in much the same way as Jesus.

In response to the question "Who is my neighbor?" John Calvin said of course we think well of our friends and family, no great surprise in that. The odd thing is that Christ commands us to love our enemies. How is that possible? Calvin answers, "All should be contemplated in God, not in themselves." If we look directly at the human race, says Calvin, unaided by God, we will feel more hate than love. We must look upon people as God looks at people. The ability not only to endure but also to love the church, small or large, arises graciously from our theological commitments. The small church is a body that only a Savior who would die for a bunch of betrayers and torturers could love. And he does.

To my suspicion that Jason gives the small church more eloquence than it deserves, I hear Jesus saying it all depends on how you look at it. Christ has a way of looking at the ragtag group of losers trotting along behind him in dusty Galilee and seeing them as disciples. He looks at that poor old compromised tart, the church, and somehow manages to see the old girl as his gloriously arrayed and virginal bride. Only a pastor who has internalized his ordination vows as well as Jason could look at the poor old small church and think *gift*.

Perhaps Jason has shown us all how to live in the small-membership church without either wanting to kill it or allowing it to kill you—*love*. Plato said that it was impossible to know anything really well without being willing to fall in love with the object of your study. Platonic epistemology is thus inherently erotic. Jason—aficionado of the wisdom of the church, devotee of the theology of Augustine, and able lover of the witness of Scripture—has also found room in his heart to look at the small church in love.

And that for me is the greatness and the challenge of Jason's book on the small church. To see our people as Christ sees them, to see the church as Christ sees it may be the one thing needful in all Christian ministry. That is what Jason Byassee has done here and that is what he so eloquently invites the rest of us to do as well.

G. K. Chesterton said that anybody who doesn't enjoy Dickens's *Pickwick Papers* (I didn't) is sure not to enjoy heaven. I think what Chesterton means is that if you won't sit with Dickens for a few hours delighting in the heights and depths of human nature, the foibles, the rich idiosyncrasies of people with their sorry sin all mixed up with their occasionally grand fidelity, there's no way you will delight at having to spend an eternity with them. To look upon God's people, not with the contempt we so richly deserve, but with the grace that God has so generously showered upon us, this is the greatest gift of all within the gift of the church that is called small.

William H. Willimon